Wealth Quotes

Seeds from the Garden

John Soforic

John Soforic/Independently Published
www.wealthybookheads.com

Publisher's Note: The publisher has nothing to note.

Book Layout © 2017 BookDesignTemplates.com

Wealth Quotes/ John Soforic. -- 1st ed.

To Patti. my wife of three
decades. Our love has always
been my greatest wealth.

Don't judge the day by the harvest your reap,
But by the seeds that you plant.

—ROBERT LOUIS STEPHENSON

Contents

Forward 1

PART I: ON TIME.. 3

Days 4

Hours 8

Weeks 14

Years 15

Time 18

PART II: ON MONEY 23

Wealth 24

Money.. 37

Prosperity 42

Rewards 46

Income 48

Spending Money.. 52

Financial Miscellaneous... 55

Riches.. 57

Saving Money 59

Debt 63

PART III: ON MIND 65

Mental Powers 66

Wealth and Focus 76

Wealth and Faith 87

Wealth and Intuition 92

Wealth and Thinking.. 97

PART IV: ON LESSONS 105

Time 106

Impact 106

Financial Dignity 107

Mental Practices 108

Challenges 108

Crisis 109

Procrastination 109

Intangible Forces 110

Wealth Seasons 110

Purpose 111

Compensation 111

Five-Year Crusades 112

Resistance 112

Productivity 113

Peak State 114

Self-Trust 115

Convictions 116

Fulfilling Work 116

Inner Values 117

Inclinations 117

Knacks 119

Ambition 119

Inner Voice 120

Courage 121

Be Unrealistic 121

Fortitude 122

Inner Circle 122

Decision 123

Sacred Efforts 123

Money Goals... 124

Schedule 125

Big Why.. 125

Gratitude 126

Certitude.. 127

Intention 127

Meditation.. 128

Mindfulness 129

Retreat.. 130

Sixth Sense 131

Discontentment.. 131

Financial Fear.. 132

Straight Edge 132

Discomfort Bridges 133

Problems... 134

Think Walks 135

Prudence... 135

Essentialism 136

Flexible Plans 137

Learning Curves 138

Self-Mastery 139

Remarkability... 139

Leverage 140

Sociability.. 140

Sour Adversity 141

Acquiescence... 142

Emotional Guidance 143

Accountability... 144

Direction 145

Self-Discipline 146

Impact Statistics 147

Asking 148

Affluence 148

Self-Forgiveness 149

Success Habits 150

Think Wealth 151

Frugality 152

Profitability.. 152

Get Out of Debt.. 153

Save Urgently 154

Keep Score 154

Minimize Risk 155

Multiply It... 156

Passive Income.. 156

PART V: ON HAPPINESS.. 159

Money and Happiness... 160

Money and Peace of Mind 165

Money and Service.. 167

More Resources.. 173

Forward

In response to requests for a quote book, here it is: *Wealth Quotes: Seeds from the Garden*. It is a collection of reader's favorite quotes and highlights. This volume contains the essential teachings of the Wealthy Gardener philosophy with lessons laid bare and exposed as raw quotes. Repetition of selected quotes has been allowed since, in essence, this is a collection of *reminders.* It is intended to be read before bed, or in the morning, to support an achievement mindset during the chaos of modern life. All quotes herein come from *The Wealthy Gardener* book except for Part IV, a bonus section on happiness. Last, the pronoun "I" used in many quotes refers to an exact phrase spoken by the Wealthy Gardener in the original book.

PART I: ON TIME

Days

Our conditions reflect our doings in the parade of passing days.

We miss the height of our fullest potential by not engaging the quiet parade of days.

You only need to fill your days with work and save every penny until something better comes along.

The seeds of all future achievement are the hours planted in passing days.

I learned that my days were the price of my aspirations, and so I gave my life to avoid the regret of lost dreams.

An unprepared mind invites suffering during the challenges of the day, but a battle-ready attitude leads to poise in turbulent conditions.

A useful life surmounts many problems, while the desire for ease causes suffering in your days.

ON TIME

I learned that a useful life was a challenging life, and a battle-ready mind-set was critical to win the day.

Dreams don't respond to the actions of someday.

Someday is an excuse to avoid the immediate discomfort and anxiety of change.

Someday leads to passive inaction, so the regrets of abandoning our dreams are not immediate.

The impossibilities of today can become the realities of tomorrow.

If you can't narrow your focus, you'll forever dissipate your potential during the crowded days of an ordinary life.

I felt steady resistance against doing the hard work of the day, but learned to conquer each task by just getting started on it.

The most productive hour of every day is the one you use to think about, imagine, dream, plan, and clarify your goals. This one hour elevates all other hours.

> *Wealth is earned by productive action in the passing days, which turn into weeks, which morph into years.*

If you want to accumulate wealth, adopt the conviction that present day sacrifices are worth future rewards.

The workday is the price we all pay to stay alive, but our free hours are the price we pay for our dreams.

Our conditions today can be traced to our past choices and actions.

The hours of today are a forecast of tomorrow.

We get only what we earn in our days. We reap what we sow.

Little good comes from prayers at night if we can't control our thoughts during the day.

We're happier when we're busy and focused on getting something we want out of our days.

Only by getting rid of the silly notion that doing less in our days leads to a better life, or that happiness and pleasure are the chief aims of living, can we come close to a useful existence that makes an impact for the common good during our brief time.

The wealthy of the future must prune the nonfruiting branches of today.

> *It is the use of days, and the impact of hours, that provides the foundation for the achievement of prosperity.*

When wealth was impractical and beyond my reach, I focused on using each day to gain steady direction.

We only have so many hours in a day, and our impact is the goal. Many adults never grasp the difference between hustling and contributing.

Tomorrow's wealthy are accumulators today. They are focused, self-disciplined, steady earners with contempt for spending. They think about wealth and what it will mean for their lives. They forgo luxuries.

What's affordable today may not be affordable tomorrow. Who has the wisdom to know the conditions of the future? Can you be sure of a steady income, good health, and prosperous times? Debtors are most harmed in an economic downturn. To free yourself of worries— free yourself of debt.

People live for the day, but they forsake the future. They haven't found the proper balance.

Hours

When I wasted my hours, I wasted my potential.

Every condition we desire, including prosperity and wealth, requires a price to be paid—our outcomes reflect our hours.

If we're busy every waking hour and getting nowhere fast, we need to change what we're doing so we use the hours better.

An impact hour is sixty minutes of doing the right things that lead to a critical outcome.

An impact hour is the opposite of a hollow hour, and it moves us forward toward our goals.

An impact hour is sixty minutes that adds to the great volume of work that is required for achievement.

Most dreams die in this plodding and action phase called work; they starve from lack of daily impact hours.

ON TIME

I saw that most dreams died from lack of daily hours, and so I rearranged my schedule for more hours of work.

We build a foundation of success by using the days, one hour at a time.

We pay the price for an extraordinary life, or the regrets of an average life. The first requires a sacrifice of our hours, but the second requires a sacrifice of our dreams.

The seeds of all future achievement are the hours planted in passing days.

If we plant only in the ordinary plot of a forty-hour workweek, we can expect to reap an ordinary harvest in our years. But if we plant in the ordinary plot and in the extraordinary plot—using the many free hours we have available each week—we give ourselves the best chance to reap an extraordinary crop in our lifetimes.

Use your hours for impact every day, but also concentrate daily on the outcomes you want most.

Problems of the day are no match for impact hours.

Money grows from the seed of desire backed by faith and ever-changing plans. And it must be kept growing with daily impact hours, or it will eventually wither and die.

I used my hours, and those hours were the key to using my full potential.

When you're starting from scratch in the middle class, upward mobility requires overtime hours and uncommon frugality.

The price of financial prosperity—the real sacrifices for abundance—is our free hours.

You must engage your hours and give your best effort every day.

> *Wealth building is nothing more than converting wasted hours into purposeful hours each day—and concentrating on your goals.*

The impact of a life always reflects the impact of its collective hours.

When I focused my attention on my goals every day, the proper attitude and actions filled up my hours.

I adopted a conviction that if I wanted to prosper, I would have to devote as many hours in each passing day as I could to productivity. And then I used my free hours to better my life.

Is daily work so hard? It is only filling hours with purpose.

The work that paid my living expenses required no willpower from me at all—this labor fed me and my family. I had no choice. It was only the use of my free hours that required any resolve.

I realized that my best life had previously been lost in the empty hours. It's a shame how many years passed without progress.

It's fun to dream, but achievement is built on hours.

Everybody is busy. But the best people not only put in more hours, they put in better hours.

Our best effort is both the quality and quantity of the hours we give to our goals.

Our Impact = right actions (work) x right intensity (effort) + right quantity (hours).

A sacred effort causes the soul to bleed. It's doing the right things in the hours, trying hard in the hours, and giving a whole lot of hours.

Decide exactly what you want in your life. I mean exactly what you cannot live without. And then decide the number of weekly hours you're willing to give to this purpose. And finally, fight for those hours as if your life depends on it.

Both prosperity and scarcity grow from the seeds of the passing hours.

With just a glance at your schedule, I can predict your future. The hours of today are a forecast of tomorrow.

ON TIME

We all have the same hours. If you can't control your schedule, you can't control your life. And if you can't make time, you need to surrender your hopes.

Hours are the building blocks of life, and unremarkable lives are built on unremarkable hours. It's just that simple.

Prosperity grows from the seeds of scheduled hours. Financial distress grows from unscheduled hours.

If change is wanted, we must change our weekly schedule.

Readjusting my schedule—my work hours and my free hours—was my perpetual attempt to regain control over my life.

I learned that success or failure grew from a schedule, and I gained direction when my hours were more valuable.

Essentialism is singular focus of hours on a concentrated purpose. It is claiming hours from the grip of the mundane. It is using time so that each day counts as progress toward a worthy cause.

Accept full accountability of your conditions. Your conditions are the sum of your waking hours.

The world is impartial to talent, brains, character, or intentions. But focus of daily hours is the equalizer of men.

It is the use of days, and the impact of hours, that provides the foundation for the achievement of prosperity.

The one with discipline will work in free hours, but the one without discipline will never be free.

We see that people can work identical hours with vastly different results. Busy is normal but impact is rare.

Wealth is an effect, the result of a valued service to mankind, built on a foundation of using the hours of many passing days.

Wealth demands effectiveness (quality hours and quantity of hours) to most fully use the days.

To win the day, use your hours with purpose.

Weeks

When a change of condition is wanted, always seek to alter the weekly schedule. Avoid hollow hours to better use the days.

Your actions reveal you. Show me your weekly schedule, and I'll tell you what you care about most in life.

The forty-hour workweek, like it or not, is a requirement of staying alive in a free-market society—not a personal sacrifice. The price of prosperity—the real sacrifice for abundance— is our free hours.

I visualized weekly outcomes and final achievements. In terms of gaining productivity, we must always confront our weekly schedule.

Don't be like a farmer who works to eat for just one week. A wise farmer schedules his days so full that his actions lead to an abundant fall harvest.

The forty-hour workweek is for survival income. We won't grow rich and prosperous from minimum efforts.

Years

If our best is not good enough this year, we can change our activities and improve our effectiveness in the upcoming season.

What's your unfinished business in this lifetime? One day you may wake up with nothing to show for the years, and it's the number one regret of the dying. Don't delay your aspirations another year.

An oak tree grows two feet a year, and the *change* is barely perceptible. But after five years, the oak will have advanced its cause by ten feet. People want to be mighty oaks without a stretch of time, but that's not the way Nature works. Every worthwhile reward or mastery of a skill grows imperceptibly over many years.

What I have found is that every five years, life changes so much that we can rarely predict what we'll want after those years have passed.

I've learned to plan my life in five-year crusades or causes—what I call magnificent bridges.

Five years is the farthest out I plan now. It's long enough for our actions to change everything, and it's a short enough span of time to manage.

Five years is short enough to be manageable but long enough to transform every unwanted condition of our lives. All of it.

The possibilities within a five-year crusade are life-changing. Why is it a crusade? Because it is a vigorous movement that transforms all.

We always have a new life every five years. And we can always choose the direction of the next five years, right now—today.

We cannot always change our unwanted condition instantly, but we can always steer in a new direction during the next five years.

I found that wanting fast results led only to despair, but a steady effort, minding my own business for five years, transforms all of life.

Anything and everything is possible with the steady use of days in a five-year crusade.

In five years, you'll be a new person with new conditions that are unrecognizable from now. I never plan farther than a five-year horizon. It will always be a new life for you every five years.

The first thirty years of life are for the learning of money. The next thirty years are for the earning of money. And the final thirty years, if done correctly, are for the burning of money.

Doubling my income during those productive years did not come from doing more or working harder; I If anything, I narrowed my focus to gainful activities. I sought simplicity. I concentrated on less.

Five years was also enough time to transform every unwanted aspect of my life through strategic plans and steady actions.

What mattered most to me was looking back at my years with satisfaction, knowing that I had nothing left in me to offer to my dreams—I had given it all. I wanted to be proud of my trying.

If you hold in your mind an amount of wealth, you'll begin to see opportunities that were there all along. It may take months or even years, but you will find the means to get it. Ideas and plans will always materialize due to your goals.

As my patience matured, I gained a reverence for five-year intervals. It was enough time to amass substantial savings; it was enough time to reap a solid return on investments; it was enough time to transform every unwanted condition of life.

Time

Without money and time, we wield little power over life.

If there is indeed a judgment in the next world, a focal question will be about the use of our time: What did we do with it? What occupied our days, weeks, and years? And won't we feel foolish to admit we were too busy and distracted to have clear goals that would have assured a greater impact in our time?

The conditions of our lives—the circumstances that surround us—are very much an accounting of how we spend that time.

Conditions reflect our purposes, effectiveness, and use of time.

Our potential is useless without our engagement of time.

> *Time is the stuff our conditions are made of.*

I saw that my conditions trail the use of my time, and I can change what I do or keep what I've got.

ON TIME

If you cannot give your free time to the pursuit of your dreams, then the seeds of achievement are not in you.

You can use your free time to pursue your dreams, or you can remain exactly where you are. And you must choose now—which will it be?

We all use the same time clock, but it is obvious that some people have more impact than others.

We make time, or we keep what we've got.

All dreams are paid for with our time. We build a foundation of success by using the days, one hour at a time.

Few goals are impossible for someone who will devote time to lifelong learning and continual self-mastery.

It is tempting to say, like the masses believe, that I sacrificed my time at a job to provide for my family. This is a delusion. The daily job is not a sacrifice because it is mandatory to one's basic survival. We must do it, even without a great cause, because we have no choice.

Time is the great tester of ideas. One's authentic pull of the inner voice is a persistent aspiration that won't die. It lasts the test of time.

Our sacrifice is found in our free time. The workday is the price we all pay to stay alive. But our free hours are the price we pay for our dreams.

In wasting time, we waste our potential.

We can only give a sacred effort in the time we're given.

Just as it takes a ship at sea a long time to change its course, so, too, does it take time to change our direction in life. But the first step takes little time. It's a slight turn of the steering wheel today.

Time and persistence are required to develop faith in our financial goals. Don't feel discouraged that it takes a span of time.

Your potential is being wasted due to how you spend your time when you do things that you know are not in line with your goals.

Your potential depends on how you engage your time.

If you can't control your time, you'll never control your conditions. And worse, you'll waste your potential. Hours are the building blocks of life, and unremarkable lives are built on unremarkable hours.

Wasting time with nothing to do is not the challenge ambitious people face in adult life. Rather, the challenge comes from doing so many mindless things that there is no time left for important things.

> *It takes time to become a success, but time is mostly what it takes.*

ON TIME

Meditation is most needed by those lacking time, for a demanding life requires daily renewal. In the stillness, we regain our center and our strength.

Time shouldn't fly—if it does, that's a sign of lazy mindlessness. When time is moving too fast, meditate to slow down the clock.

Cut the frivolous and mundane pursuits that waste time. Focus your power.

Essentialism is a narrow focus on one thing, the use of energy and time on a sole task. It requires saying no to almost everything and saying yes to just a few things.

Observe the fate of the one who lives only for the day. He lets time pass without impact, and in turn allows a life without significance.

A person's time on Earth can be compared to a plot of ground. It exists; it's there. It has within itself an astonishing potential, and it's prepared to react to a person's every action. In fact, it must. Each of us is given a plot to work, a lifetime, and the work we have chosen. Like a farmer, we can be grateful if we have the vision, imagination, and intelligence to successfully build upon the seemingly unimpressive land of our beginnings. Or we can let it fall into a haphazard condition with no real continuity of purpose behind it, with unpainted, ramshackle buildings, surrounded by weeds and debris. In both cases, the land is the same; it's what we do with it that makes the difference. The potential for a miracle is there, if only we're wise enough to see it and to realize that our fulfillment as people depends upon our reaction to what we've been given.

ON TIME

Woe to the one who wastes time and then defends aimlessness. His alibis secure his future regrets.

The wealthy tend to narrow their aims and direct their time and effort. They avoid mindless pursuits because they want money and the lifestyle it can afford them.

In your quiet time, assure yourself that wealth is your destiny. Feel prosperous until it feels natural. Drive wealth deep into your mind. Build a faith that displaces all doubts.

Wealth finds those who clearly know what they want—and why they want it—and spend a lot of time thinking about it.

Time wasted is money lost and wealth abandoned.

Wealth demands sacrifice. I accepted that I could not have it all, and so I chose between having money or time. I opted to sacrifice my time to amass wealth. And when I had wealth, I had lots of time.

Life is a competition, and your opponent is time. And the clock is ticking—until it is done ticking for you. Always know that you—not fate or circumstances—determine the final score against time.

PART II: ON MONEY

Wealth

Wealth grows from the seeds of desire.

Unlike a tree that grows on its own, your wealth tree is happy to not grow at all.

Building wealth is a drama that unfolds in three distinct acts. The growth of financial prosperity has a spring, a summer, and a fall.

Wealth grows in stride with our competence. Indeed, wealth is a mistress who is attracted only to those with personal power.

The storybook fantasy is that the climb to wealth is a glamorous ascent. The reality is a journey of sacrifice and inconvenience backed by a cause more important than your personal comforts.

Wealth flows from a useful service that loves us back.

On Money

Like a sculptor with rare vision, the seeker of wealth needs extraordinary resolve to achieve riches. You must always trust the vision that was placed in your heart, and know you can achieve it.

Most people who say excess money is wrong really don't want to work too hard, sacrifice, or be inconvenienced to amass it.

It is practical to choose fulfilling employment, because wealth requires stamina over the course of many years.

What makes you unlike anyone else on this planet is the unique mix of your values, inclinations, knacks, ambition, and inner voice. Any effective wealth strategy begins with discovering your best qualities and then applying those assets to good work.

The secret of your fullest wealth is using your individuality.

Ambition for wealth is a natural tendency toward security and personal freedom. It is personal drive, desire, determination, and motivation. It is the will to work hard—sometimes even an inability to not work hard—for a personal dream or aspiration.

Wealth is a reward that is reserved for those who add value to the common good.

In wealth building, ambition without caution is a bus without brakes, but ambition without courage is a bus without keys.

Wealth favors the individual with courage and caution in the right measure.

Accumulating wealth requires defining moments of weighing the consequences of action against the dangers of inaction.

Wealth follows draining journeys, and the quest must endure after inspiration has fled. It's for the finishers, not the starters.

Wealth requires a selective, well-chosen inner circle—with a guard at the door to prevent the negative influence of others. A friendship with a fool can be a costly affair.

Wealth favors the one whose decisions are influenced by clear goals and are visible in execution.

We leave our wealth to chance by failing to set financial goals.

Our daily schedule determines who we become, what we earn, and how much wealth we can amass in our lifetimes.

You will encounter inevitable adversities and obstacles— the storms of life—in your achievement cycle. Having a big why during these times allows you to withstand the storms.

Your compelling reason for wealth is like the roots of a tree that keep it anchored and assure its survival despite the weather.

On Money

The accumulation of paper is nothing. What the paper will do for you and how it will serve you—that is what sustains the fight.

People need a reason to choose wealth over ease. We all wage a daily struggle against resistance. Without a big why, people naturally procrastinate, make excuses, avoid sacrifices, and don't follow through with their plans.

A big why will be the cause of your persistence.

A compelling purpose for wealth provides the drive you need to overcome the odds.

If it's fun you're after, a goal of wealth isn't for you. But if it's freedom you need, the sacrifice is worth it.

Your fortune is either worth it or not, depending on why you want it.

Our reasons for wealth ensure our persistence.

> *Wealth requires either willpower or why power, and the latter is often the real source of the former.*

A big why pushes us, regardless of our mood, energy, state of mind, or even attitude. A big why may be the welfare of a family, paid college education, or freedom from debt. It may be the fear of losing a job, an escape from wage slavery, or the end of financial insecurity.

We control little more than our daily intentions, but intention is the conductor of our wealth affairs.

Scarcity cannot long survive in a mind of rich thoughts.

A state of wealth consciousness is a feeling of success with certainty of prosperity. Riches grow from rich thoughts.

Those who desire wealth must accept uncertainty and vulnerability. We must forever choose ambition over comfort, effort over ease, exertions over excuses, and contribution over complacency.

I found that wealth required walking into discomfort, and so I crossed bridges of discomfort to get a better life.

Wealth requires strategic thinking with a calm respect for the worst consequences. Those without prudence often learn the pain of misjudgments.

Wealth rewards a narrow focus on potent activities.

If wealth be the goal, get your mind off distractions and onto your one thing. Those who acquire wealth in the future must prune the nonfruiting branches today.

Work, work, and more work—like your life depends on it—on things that produce monthly savings. If that seems like too much, wealth is not for you. And neither is any other worthy achievement.

The road to wealth has many detours and setbacks along the way, and that is why riches require a fixed goal with flexible plans.

On Money

The only certainty on the road to wealth is that you will need to constantly improvise plans. You will meet with setbacks, and you'll make mistakes, but you can always change your strategy.

Keep your mind on wealth throughout every day—focus on being the successful person who already owns it.

My upward mobility relied on my daily capacity to hold a clear goal of wealth in my mind and to believe I would achieve it despite all evidence to the contrary.

The way to wealth is a steady forward direction, which happens to be the way to life satisfaction.

The fall harvest unfolds when our thoughts are filled with purpose and faith. Opportunities will arise that you cannot imagine.

With clarity and trust, the seeds of wealth will grow in the right seasons.

Saving a dollar each day, trivial as it may seem, had a transformative effect on me. This simple act developed my wealth consciousness.

When wealth was impractical and beyond my reach, I focused on using each day to gain steady direction.

Wealth requires sacrifices, but mediocrity requires insecurity.

I wondered if wealth required too much sacrifice, until I saw that mediocrity required too much worry.

Wealth is built on results, and it grows from steady impact that can be measured in the passing days.

Wealth arises from consistent, result-producing efforts that can be measured. These impact activities can be tracked in hours, while other inputs are best tracked by tasks completed.

Wealth arises from passing sacrifices that yield rewards.

Wealth grows from the smallest advantages.

We hear people complaining that the rich get richer, but these complainers are failing to earn their own small advantages.

Wealth is power. With wealth many things are possible.

Wealth expands options.

What most people never suspect, is that wealth involves a lot of personal mistakes, wrong choices, and even public humiliations.

Most people who achieve wealth have a humbler lifestyle. They are accumulators, not big spenders. They are focused on the long game.

Thinking of wealth leads to behaviors that lead to accumulation.

Regardless of the causes behind it, what we think about tends to become our reality. The outer world is but a reflection of our inner world. This has been the constant truth of my life.

Wealth tends to elude any person, regardless of income, who does not make wealth a priority.

People who eventually gain wealth think a lot about it.

Keep a vision of wealth close to your heart. Write goals and read them at night and in the morning. Feel amassed money in your possession and see yourself performing services to earn this reward.

In solitude, assure yourself that wealth is your destiny. Feel prosperous until it feels natural. Drive wealth deep into your mind. Build a faith that displaces all doubts.

The days pass and, with focus, your wealth will grow.

Thinking of wealth will influence the mind to make better choices.

The wealthy must want wealth more than they want comfort, luxury, or social status.

Wealth finds those who clearly know what they want—and why they want it—and spend a lot of time thinking about it.

Since I tended to get what I thought about in life, I concentrated daily on wealth and why I wanted it.

Wealth is built on profit-*ability*. It's the ability to earn money and spend money in a way that results in excess money to save.

Wealth won't grow from minimum efforts. Accumulation requires sacrifice—working smarter, harder, and longer—and this explains its rarity. More income may require working two jobs, pursuing more education to increase earning capacity, or running a side business.

Gaining wealth is a marathon made up of consistently saving small amounts—all the days of our lives—to one day gain access to the banquet of ownership. And once we gain access to opportunities, we gain financial advantages.

Tracking your net worth lets you see the direction of your wealth during your marathon of accumulating money.

The origin of all wealth is initially the ability to stash money in the bank. But engaging those dollars effectively requires a fierce competition with inflation.

The challenge of wealth has little to do with the complexity of investing. Those who get wealthy focus on their behaviors.

Wealth unfolds begrudgingly like the slow growth of an oak tree.

On Money

Wealth is the consistent effect of working to earn, followed by urgently saving and investing all excess money over many years. I saw that fretting never makes money grow, but wealth multiplies best with enduring patience.

The ultimate goal of wealth is security and personal liberty.

Wealth is a river of income that flows generously on its own.

The reason to strive for prosperity and wealth is to be able to one day pursue more important purposes than making money.

A purpose for wealth, beyond hoarding it, is vital to sustain the ongoing persistence needed to acquire it.

The power of self-trust is integral to wealth, because in life we get the poorest conditions we will tolerate.

If you want to accumulate wealth, the ritual of daily mental practices is valuable, but don't neglect your duties. Adopt the belief that you will concentrate on your desires and cultivate faith in your goals, but also give a sacred effort to uphold your part of the bargain.

Wealth, possessed by good people, is peace of mind, lifestyle satisfaction, family protection, financial security, and power.

Are you willing to trade your current freedom temporarily for the ultimate freedom of time and money later in life?

On Money

Spending is the enemy of amassing a fortune.

Accumulators live without an ostentatious display of money or luxuries. They gravitate to the simplest pleasures that are free.

I didn't know how I would amass enough money to reach my financial dreams, but I chose to believe that I was destined for wealth, so I'd figure it out, and be aided by Universal Intelligence along the way when I concentrated on my goals with absolute faith.

I chose to believe that I could influence my belief that I'd be wealthy. And wealth has unfolded—as I chose to believe.

Countless are the plans that can lead to wealth, and varied are the traits of the workers who can earn it.

If we want wealth, we must work where money is likely to exist in abundance.

I thought rugged determination was the way to wealth, but learned to work ruggedly within my own unique set of interests.

I found that my inner circle had to change to achieve wealth, but what was lost in quantity was offset by rare quality.

If you hold in your mind an amount of wealth, you'll begin to see opportunities that were there all along. It may take months or even years, but you will find the means to get it. Ideas and plans will always materialize due to your goals.

I will try to avoid being redundant, but wealth, for me—the core of the matter—was foremost about learning to control my thoughts.

The masses may want wealth, but their desires compete with many other wants.

The accumulation of money comes to those who seek it and sacrifice their contradictory desires. It eludes those with scattered focus.

Accumulation of wealth, before actions and choices that lead to it, requires uncommon thinking.

Saving money now is the way to wealth, while saving someday is the way to scarcity.

Net worth is a single snapshot of your wealth, and its moving parts, frozen in time.

Guarding your mind against the negative influence of others is a skill you must acquire to become wealthy. The negativity of others has stolen many a fortune.

If you want to be wealthy, the use of excess money is never a decision for the whims of your desires. All surplus money must be saved to build your financial prosperity.

To become wealthy, we must transition from consumers into owners and investors. Ownership of stocks, bonds, real estate, a business— this is the way to wealth.

Without savings, the banquet of ownership is not for you. With enough savings, the doors open. And so, too, do the opportunities.

Money

Many things are indeed more important than money, but overcoming the 'money problem' allows us to focus on these more important things.

Without money and time, we wield little power over life.

When we're faced with a problem that money can solve and we have the money to solve it, then we face a trivial problem. But lacking this money, even the smallest of life's problems can turn into the worst of life's problems.

Money, like oxygen, is not too important until there is not enough of it. But when levels run low, every waking hour is consumed by it— either spent working for money or worrying about it.

I learned that lack of money erodes self-respect, and a noble dignity arises by earning a living.

An income equal to living expenses is precarious, and the pursuit of excess money is wise and necessary.

On Money

You may want to consider that while you're living with your parents, you could save more money from an ordinary job than you've saved throughout your adult working life. You only need to fill your days with work and save every penny until something better comes along.

I have witnessed unrewarded struggles for money, and it is as common as unanswered prayers for money. Begging is a fool's game.

My own success required hard work and daily mental practices. Both contributed to my economic fate.

Money grows from the seed of desire backed by faith and ever-changing plans.

it's not about how much money we earn that counts, but how much we save.

Start with a goal of prosperity—and I mean an exact amount of money—and give it a completion date. Then grow to be worthy of it.

Expand your mind until you no longer fit into your current environment. You will then witness that all gardens grow from the mind of the gardener. The way to a larger garden is to outgrow the one you've got. Set impossible goals, and then apply yourself to activities that impact the realization of those goals.

Money itself may not be enough to motivate us to sacrifice but sending kids to college may get us moving. Escaping poverty or debt may be reason enough to give up our leisure time. The dream of freedom can inspire us to work harder and amass wealth. We are wired to seek a life of purpose and forward direction. When we discover what makes us tick, we discover our full power.

A deeper cause fuels the persistence behind the sacrifices of achievement—including the amassing of wealth and freedom.

Decide how much money you desire and why you want it, and focus on both daily. This is not an option if you want wealth.

If you can imagine wealth with absolute faith that you will have it, and if you can maintain this mindset for as long as it takes, then everything else will work out. You'll be guided by your inner wisdom.

We leave our finances to fate if we fail to set money goals.

I discovered magic in the daily review of money goals, and this new practice attuned me to opportunities that were previously unseen.

It's easier to work for money than it is to worry about money.

Work is always easier than worry. Worry kills us, not hard work.

An emotional mind makes mistakes, while a rational mind makes money. Let passion give way to reason when dreaming gives way to planning.

On Money

The molder of internal conditions is the shaper of external conditions. We master our money by mastering ourselves.

We control money by controlling ourselves.

I learned to master my intentions, emotions, and actions—and by controlling myself, I gained control over money.

You must acquire excess money and use it to grow your own advantages.

Smart money always seeks a home. You will always find eager investors if you can ensure the safety of their money and show them a successful track record of your own responsible behaviors.

The ultimate blessing of having enough money is never having to worry about having enough money. Peace of mind is priceless.

Discipline will wane when the climbing gets steep, but a compelling purpose for the money fortifies our determination.

The accumulation of money comes to those who seek it and sacrifice their contradictory desires.

The key to my wealth? It's simple—the stuff I own earns money.

An automated savings plan works because it imposes an artificial environment of scarcity. With little money to spend, we clearly choose our needs—not our wants. And somehow, we manage to always survive while saving money.

Wealth is mostly about spending. No matter how much money people earn, they tend to spend the entire amount and a little bit more besides. Their expenses rise in lockstep with their incomes. Many people today earn several times what they earned at their first jobs. But somehow they seem to need every single penny to maintain their current lifestyles. No matter how much they make, there never seems to be enough. It explains why most people are broke.

The only thing easy about money is losing it. Keep that in mind when you're feeling infallible.

I thought money grew by its annual rate of return, but found that it only grows by how much it beats inflation.

When we are broke, we must give our life to create a money snowball that grows on its own. But in time the money becomes a genie that has no equal for granting wishes.

Prosperity

The rewards of prosperity are found in the work, the freedom, and the personal growth so necessary to attain uncommon wealth.

Prosperity is the power to take a walk in the woods on a weekday, pay for college tuitions, and live with choices, options, and peace. It is waking up without money worries, and living without time pressure.

I was told that ambition for riches comes from the devil, but found that the prosperous life was a spiritual adventure.

Striving for prosperity is the natural desire to be free.

The price of financial prosperity—the real sacrifices for abundance—is found in our free hours.

Prosperity requires sustained inconveniences, so we must be driven to gain it by causes greater than our desire for comfort.

We can save one dollar and steer toward prosperity. We can always do one thing. Crusades are made of direction and deeper causes.

On Money

A prosperous life is a productive life, and productivity leads to a smile of satisfaction at the end of many long days of steady contribution.

> Our lives are not determined by what we want, but by what we will accept and tolerate. If we want financial freedom but will accept financial stability—a good job that pays the bills—we will get the latter. If we want prosperity but will accept financial struggles in the middle class, we will live and retire in the middle class. If we want abundance but will accept mediocrity, it is certain that our fate will be one of mundane struggles.

Do not ask, "What should I do with my life?" Ask, "What individual values must I fulfill in my life's pursuits?" This question leads to a more fulfilling journey toward prosperity.

If you pursue prosperity, ethically and without hurting others, it is a driving force that assures a worthwhile contribution in your life.

You don't gain prosperity because you have clarity of goals. You get only what you earn in your days. You reap what you sow.

Prosperity requires uncommon persistence, but your willpower is assured by your why power.

Unwanted conditions can break the spirit of the masses, but the winners of prosperity use aggravations to fuel their advancements.

The moral is to face your problems and use your fullest potential to stage a rebellion. Be the exception of an oppressed population by creating a lifestyle of prosperity for which there is no need to escape.

The prosperous life is a brave life. All worthy achievements require a walk into likely discomforts—and admirable sacrifices.

The prosperous life requires a walk into fear, uncertainty, discomfort, and temporary inconveniences. It's not for pleasure-seekers.

Prosperity requires saying no to almost everything, and saying yes to only a few things.

The people who win prosperity give their strength, energy, and attention to just one fruit—their personal net worth.

I gained prosperity despite setbacks and misfortunes, by being stubborn about goals and flexible about plans.

Meeting expectations earns us a living, but surpassing expectations earns us prosperity.

The prosperous seek negotiations, and realize that options equal power. Leverage is the ability to award benefits, impose losses, or walk away from a compromise.

We are all self-made, but only the prosperous admit it.

One's conditions are the grade of one's past.

Trust prosperity to grow, knowing that plans always spring from a conditioned mind. The abundant fall harvest unfolds when our thoughts are filled with purpose and faith.

On Money

Poverty and financial insecurity are no match for consistent steps on a prosperous pathway.

It is the use of days, and the impact of hours, that provides the foundation for the achievement of prosperity.

Prosperity may be a way of life, but it's a way of life that's built on doing the right things. The longer we do the right things, the more these right things become our habitual patterns.

I erred in thinking that habits were for weaklings, but saw that my own prosperity was built on daily habits.

Feel prosperous until it feels natural. Drive wealth deep into your mind. Build a faith that displaces all doubts.

Rewards

There is never a certainty of future rewards, but we must go for it anyway, or keep what we've got.

We get crowned with uncommon rewards only after we stretch beyond our realistic expectations.

Uncommon rewards are available to those who can pass the test of uncommon sacrifice and persistence. It's not for common people.

Self-actualization, and the accumulation of riches, is the ultimate reward of life impossible for comfort seekers.

The way to our fullest potential always involves bridges of discomfort. And every bridge is only a temporary passageway that leads to a reward on the other side.

God made the tough paths lead to the greatest rewards. And you will be happier on the tough paths. The hardest path of all is beaten path. It is struggle, worry, lack of hope, and little reward beyond getting by.

On Money

I saw that only a few actions earned tangible monetary rewards, and so I rearranged my schedule for more of the best activities.

You must earn what you get, and your rewards will always be a true indicator of the service you give.

Your work should reward you with satisfaction, it should fulfill a need within you to contribute in your own way, and it should pay you enough money to support the lifestyle you desire.

Over time, unrewarded effort breeds resentment. The right service [livelihood] for you is the one that loves you back.

I never enjoyed the daily pain during the years I built my wealth, but I was rewarded by conquering it. The pain ends, and the rewards stay.

Income

An income equal to living expenses is a precarious situation.

Without more than enough income, we exist like caged birds, trapped without choices in a state of limitations.

An income without more than enough is not nearly enough. Only a fool aims for survival without excess.

I doubled my income by engaging in impact activities. Some of those activities were mental practices that I didn't reveal to even my closest friends. I concentrated daily on picturing my wishes fulfilled. And I generated emotion as I imagined the life of my dreams. I also worked a lot, too. All of it came together to produce the income.

An important income results from important contributions.

In a free market society, we receive an income only by offering a valuable service or product to help others.

Our income reflects the need for our service, how well we perform it, how difficult it would be to replace us, and how many people we serve. These four factors are the income formula.

It requires no more than a click on a computer or cell phone to determine the top-earning jobs, careers, and occupations. Within seconds, we can see what income each job, career, or occupation earns. Is it wrong to start with a search of top incomes and figure out which job we like the most, based, in part, on those search results?

When choosing a career, the "income down" approach worked well for my best friend who became an orthodontist. He didn't start with a passion for straightening teeth. He started by looking at top paying careers. And his annual income has quadrupled mine every week despite working only half the weekly hours as me.

Income level, more than any other factor, determines the ease of upward mobility. Some jobs are more valuable to the marketplace, and therefore two people working the same number of hours in different jobs can find themselves in dissimilar financial situations.

A life of small problems produces a small income.

The rich may get richer, but only because they once managed their income and expenses to gain an advantage.

I had to earn financial advantages by managing my income and expenses, and then I managed my advantages to amass my wealth.

Substantial wealth tends to elude any person, regardless of income, who does not make wealth a priority.

> *We see high-income earners consuming 'prestige products.' But the more visible their spending, the less likely they're saving.*

Most people, regardless of other factors, tend to raise their spending to their incomes. It explains why so few people end up with wealth.

In the end, people tend to give away all income. This tendency is especially prevalent among high-earners with status jobs. If you have little to save from each paycheck, you are giving it all away.

With a leaky dam, water cannot accumulate despite the generous flow of the river. Likewise, a lifetime of income without frugality always depletes.

More income may require working two jobs, pursuing more education to increase earning capacity, or running a side business. Or it may just require more hours where you are right now.

Keep your mortgage under twice your annual realized income. And, as for cars, you don't need one that costs over $30,000.

Passive income is the aim of those who dream of freedom. It's the profits, cash flow, and earnings that do not require involvement from an owner. It's the mythical river of gold.

The goal of passive income was not idleness; it was choices and options for a richer, fuller life.

Passive income is cash flow with little or no effort required—it is time freedom.

Passive income is personal liberty.

Rental property income tends to be the most common road to passive income for average people with ordinary incomes.

When a million dollars is needed for an annual retirement income of $30,000, ambitious middle-class people tend to become creative with limited resources.

Wealth is a river of income that flows generously on its own.

Spending Money

Spending is thrilling at times, but it decreases financial stability.

If I didn't control the outflow of money, then my life would be vulnerable to calamities.

Trying to amass wealth without tightfisted spending is like trying to fill a bathtub without plugging the drain—it is the insanity of adult self-indulgence.

Spending is the enemy of amassing a fortune.

It is a virtue to live below our means without an ostentatious display of wealth or extravagant luxuries. The best things in life are the simplest pleasures.

It's up to each of us to choose how we spend our justly earned money. Who can say what's wrong for the earnings of another?

For any hope of wealth in the future, we need to earn income, control spending, and save money.

On Money

Most people who achieve wealth have a humble lifestyle. They are big accumulators, not big spenders. They don't care about looking wealthy, but they do care a lot about being wealthy.

Tomorrow's wealthy are the accumulators of today. They are focused, self-disciplined, steady earners with contempt for spending.

We can only see spending—not bank accounts. Wealth is invisible in the real world. We only see spending. And the more visible the spending, the less likely it is that they're saving.

Spending is fun, but frugality leads to freedom.

Spending is instantly gratifying, but it can lead to wage slavery.

Luxury cars and expensive homes come at a price—they deplete wealth.

I faced daily choices between spending or saving, and gained upward mobility through sacrifice and modesty.

In a business, an owner who spends profits on luxuries will usually end in failure. In life, the same tendency causes under accumulation.

Spending money on nonessential items leads to vulnerability. We need to stash our excess money to one day be wealthy.

Household economy is the first issue to resolve. It takes a good offense, or earning more, and it takes a good defense, or spending less.

We need to set aside a portion of every paycheck to create a condition of forced scarcity. This plan reduces our capacity to spend. It is the way to assure the behaviors that lead to wealth.

When we exist in an environment of economic scarcity, it ensures our frugality. With little money to spend, we choose our needs—not our wants. And somehow, we manage to always survive just fine.

Spending is the cause of failure.

Paying yourself first will create a spending constraint to assure your monthly profitability.

Without urgency to save, we spend arbitrarily and then wonder where the money goes.

Save at the start of each month using an automatic savings draft from every paycheck. Such a plan will create a sustainable structure for spending while you accumulate wealth; it ensures progress without willpower. Since you can't spend what you don't see, it's important to move the money into the bank before you have access to it.

When you're starting from scratch in the middle class, upward mobility requires overtime hours and uncommon frugality.

Everybody wants a cure for financial problems, but nobody likes the medicine. Frugality is the medicine.

Financial Miscellaneous

Ambition for wealth is about gaining the upper hand, not over others, but over life's financial condition.

The dream was to live with no economic concerns and, ultimately, experience a fuller life through financial freedom.

I was a wage slave. And I determined that to win my freedom, I would need to succeed financially. I'd win, or a part of me would die.

Poverty and financial insecurity are no match for consistent steps on a prosperous pathway.

My journey to financial freedom was a course of misses, blunders, surprises, humility, setbacks, mistakes, misjudgments, missed goals, and slim escapes from financial disasters. We adapt or we perish.

Wicked storms and financial setbacks happen in every life, but the real problems occur when misfortunes become excuses.

Self-mastery is a lot of things. But we are talking about financial success, and so it's about an obsessive devotion to our goals.

Your financial security is about what makes you remarkable compared to the competition. Give people a reason to remark about you.

Until you're like a tractor to a farmer, you'll have no financial security. You have leverage only when others fear losing you.

Financial security is gained with quality options. If you have no options, you are stuck. With quality options, you are free.

Your job is to always increase your financial options. What can you do to build new skills, be more valuable, or increase your knowledge?

I struggled in vain to influence financial outcomes, until I saw that options are the leverage in negotiations. If I had to agree to terms, I was screwed from the start. The option to walk away is leverage.

It is crucial to note that every major financial advancement during my life has followed a bold question. There were always many other factors involved, but these other factors varied according to the situation. The only constant in these life-changing leaps of progress was a bold question. Bold asking always preceded every big break.

Riches

If you desire riches, guard your mind against the susceptibility to negative influences. And focus on your most coveted goal.

Scarcity cannot long survive in a mind of rich thoughts.

A state of wealth consciousness is a feeling of success with certainty of prosperity. Riches grow from rich thoughts.

> *Rule number one is that you will not get the richest condition you want, but the poorest condition you will accept.*

There is no such thing as success without aggravations, and riches gravitate to those who solve the big problems.

It is self-control, detached objectivity, and practical calculation that leads to steady financial direction and a richer life.

All earned riches require a fixed goal with flexible plans.

Any fifth grader can grasp the strategies required to be rich. It is human behavior that leads to failure of the masses.

The gathering of riches requires actions and choices that are compatible with its buildup.

> *Rich people stay rich by living like they are broke; broke people stay broke by living like they are rich.*

I can't promise that saving money will make you fabulously rich, but it will make you happier and richer. I can promise you that much.

Saving Money

In the old days, a person who saved money was a miser; nowadays, the same person is a wonder.

You may want to consider that while you're living with your parents, you could save more money from an ordinary job than you've saved throughout your adult working life. You only need to fill your days with work and save every penny until something better comes along.

> *My financial breaks were due to a lot of small things along the way, none of which would have happened without saving money.*

It's not how much money we earn that counts, but how much we save. We can save one dollar and steer toward prosperity.

There is no worse enemy for our profitability than debt, and without profits, there is nothing to save and no hope for wealth.

Smart people without savings are worried people. Dumb people don't think about it. With savings, this worry condition improves.

If we make ten dollars and spend nine, we obviously have one dollar to save. Most people know the simple math, and yet this extra dollar always finds a home far away. People always spend without saving.

In modern times, we may need to accept that we can't save money working a forty-hour job.

Not amassing savings is our fault. We allow it all, and we must own it all. When we blame others, or the conditions surrounding us, or any external factor, we give up our power to change.

If you want to be wealthy, the use of excess money is never a decision for the whims of your desires. All surplus is saved to build your financial prosperity.

Anyone who advises against saving money is a fool to be disregarded for further advice.

> *To become wealthy, you must transition from consumer into owner and investor. Ownership is the way to wealth. It is the only way to wealth. Without savings, this option is not for you. With enough savings, the doors open. You can be an owner.*

I saved urgently—and it made all the difference. The others knew they should save, but it wasn't urgent for them. And without urgency, their attention was on other things until it was too late.

My friends got caught up in their everyday lives. They failed to save money because retirement seemed so far away—until it wasn't.

Saving urgently means banking excess income as the top priority. Without urgency to save, we spend arbitrarily and then wonder where the money goes.

Saving urgently is vital because an empty bank account causes hopelessness, vulnerability, and dependence. Worse, it causes smart people to fear losing thankless jobs they hate.

Saving money provides a cushion against catastrophe. It is the power to absorb hard punches.

Gaining wealth is a marathon made up of consistently saving small amounts—all the days of our lives—to one day gain access to the banquet of ownership.

Save each month using an automatic savings draft from every paycheck. Such a plan will create a sustainable structure for spending while you accumulate wealth; it ensures progress without willpower.

Saving now is the way to wealth, while saving someday is the way to scarcity.

Keep working, keep saving, keep investing, keep repeating. These are the gears of our wealth.

Wealth is the consistent effect of working to earn, followed by urgently saving and investing all excess money over many years.

Steady savings will multiply wealth in unimaginable ways, and we multiply wealth not just by saving, but by planting seeds and leaving them alone.

According to a safe retirement rule of thumb, we can withdraw three percent annually from our amassed savings.

How much will you need to save for retirement? It depends on your desired retirement income. Figure out how much income you'll want in retirement, and multiply it by 25 as a general rule.

Saving money must be urgent, and then investments must be given patience without interference or meddling.

It was a sacrifice to save money while others spent lavishly on possessions, but I was rewarded with the satisfaction of my growing security, options, and freedom. There is joy in direction.

> *if luck is when opportunity meets preparation, then preparation is a pile of cash when opportunity knocks.*

I saw that an empty bank account left me powerless, but a pile of cash offered security and possibilities.

The goal of investing hard-earned cash, before any thought of gains, is always about the avoidance of its departure.

Debt

Debt robs the future of time and money. It chains the worker to the wages.

Debtors come to realize that their futures have been sold to their creditors.

When monthly wages are consumed by debt payments, the soul always grows weary.

Debtors are most harmed in an economic downturn.

To free yourself of worries—free yourself of debt.

Every time you pay off a debt, you have that much more to pay off other debts and, in the end, to eventually save toward your wealth.

Debt robs the future to pay for the wants of today.

Debtors suffer the pain of sacrifice or the pain of slavery.

Debt is a cruel master who accrues interest while we sleep.

If you ever want freedom, you must break free of debt. It is the slave master in a free society, the obligator of drudgery.

I realized that debt enslaved me to duty, but a life without debt was a life without chains.

Get the small wins, and each paid debt will increase your free cash to pay off remaining debts.

PART III: ON MIND

Mental Powers

It's possible that we know very little of our mental potential; It seems much is yet to be learned about a human mind fixated on a clear aim.

We become what we think about. Energy flows where attention goes. Hold a goal within you, and everything will take care of itself.

Within the mind lay the solutions to overcome the worst economic hardships. Scarcity cannot long survive in a mind of rich thoughts.

If goals are magnets, then certitude is the magnetism.

Keep your mind on wealth throughout every day—focus on being the successful person who already owns it. Feel wealthy to be wealthy.

When I was at my best in this world, the skies opened and rained uncanny breaks, inspirations, coincidences, and rare opportunities upon me. My good fortune was not all from my own hands. But then again, without the work of my own hands, I would have surely died in a drought instead of prospering. I worked hard, but also sensed an Unseen Force working with me, beside me, and through me.

You must start with the dream, maintain it in your mind, dwell on it, and let the how catch up to it. And then be forever cynical of realistic expectations.

I've trusted hard work to earn my success. But in private, I've also trusted daily mental practices to earn my good luck.

Financial security has always been the effect of an Intangible Force— a power within, a certainty of outcome, an absurd kind of faith.

Don't ever speak lightly of Intangible Forces. When you doubt the unknown, you doubt yourself. You have more potential within you than a tiny acorn, and the Unseen Power is available to help grow your individuality into its fullest expression.

If you hold in your mind an amount of wealth, you'll begin to see opportunities that were there all along. It may take months or even years, but you will find the means to get it.

We gain the cooperation of Intangible Forces when we emotionally feel an outcome in our imagination. We produce serendipity and synchronicity according to the depth of our faith.

Once a goal takes root in the mind and we gain faith surrounding its attainment, the world slowly changes—and coincidences show up.

Goals backed by faith led to the illumination of opportunities that were previously unnoticed.

67

Be reverent of the things you find fascinating and enthralling. Your unique fascinations expose the inclinations, tendencies, interests, and proclivities hidden deep in the substance of your intangible soul.

Gardeners are not afraid of working hard to shape the landscape, but they are also aware of a mysterious Unseen Force that operates behind the scenes to make the plants grow.

I believe miracles are natural phenomena of a cause and effect that Nature has not yet revealed to us. I've seen evidence of an Unseen Force that responds to goals and faith.

The Unseen Force works to aid the fullest expression of life. You can use this power, or you can struggle alone. The Force is indifferent.

In addition to my own efforts, I discovered powers of my mind, and this skill catapulted me in big leaps. I worked with the Unseen Force that aided my efforts according to my faith.

Your mind is the Unseen Power, the essence of your potential, the core of your being. You control it, or you control nothing.

A controlled mind is the force that compels the actions, choices, work, and struggles behind every worthy achievement. You have a Godlike potential in your mind, and you are accountable for it above all else. You honor it, or you waste it. And your conditions reveal your mind.

On Mind

We work in concert with a Silent Power that aids our wealth and manifests things in mysterious ways. And many people, without realizing it, are using this power unwittingly due to their faith.

If Universal Intelligence is a delusion, then focusing on goals, cultivating faith, developing plans, offering hours, and living with purpose can only help us achieve our dreams. And we may observe a few coincidences that expand our closed minds.

I have learned through experience that Universal Intelligence is working when inspirations begin to flow and uncanny coincidences start to show up in harmony with my most dominant thoughts.

I believe in Universal Intelligence. When I feel something isn't quite right in life, I meditate for an answer. I imagine that my limited intelligence can gain access to an infinite intelligence.

I found that the inner voice whispers in the silence, and that Universal Intelligence will aid financial ambitions.

You need to develop a cause, a meaning, to keep you going through hard times. And you must learn to live in a world that you can't see but can sense, forever knowing that you are never alone because you're a part of the Universal Intelligence.

Most people will never be wealthy because of their convictions that too much work is misguided, that the aid of Universal Intelligence is a delusion, or that too much wealth is wrong or immoral. They won't realize their full wealth potential due to these limiting beliefs.

I choose to believe in a real-life matrix governed not by machines but by Universal Intelligence. I choose to believe this regulating force of the matrix is not oppressive but rather cooperative with our goals. And I choose to believe I can tap into this matrix force through daily concentration and applied faith.

At the age of thirty, I didn't know how I would amass enough money to reach my financial dreams, but I chose to believe that I was destined for wealth, so I'd figure it out, and be aided by Universal Intelligence along the way when I concentrated on my goals with absolute faith.

Cling to your goal in faith, and Universal Intelligence will hand over the plan. It never fails—it is a law of Nature.

Where do aspirations originate? It seems that the inner voice resonates with something deep within the Universal Intelligence that governs this world.

With gratitude, we trigger Universal Intelligence to help our cause.

With gratitude, we speak the language of Universal Intelligence and ask for an assist—even if our purpose is material wealth.

I was open-minded enough to trust that Universal Intelligence would notice if I stirred up a burning gratitude for an outcome.

Self-mastery engages the aid of the Universal Intelligence.

On Mind

When I look at a dormant acorn, I am reminded of its potential, and I am humbled by the mysteries of the Universal Intelligence beyond my understanding.

You have within your mind that potential of Universal Intelligence to shape your conditions.

Universal Intelligence always responds to clarity and faith.

Your consciousness is a marvel, the miracle of all-time. What unfathomable Silent Force is behind serendipity and synchronicity? Who can deny the wonder of Universal Intelligence in a garden?

In nature we see the cooperative energy all around us, or at least we see the effects of it. We don't see the wind, but we see the rustling leaves. We see the effects of an Intangible Force in every garden— the same power that exists in our lives, that governs all of it.

We gain the cooperation of a Silent Partner in the quest for wealth if we know what we want, maintain absolute faith, offer many impact hours, and heed the whispers.

I've found that my own success required hard work and daily mental practices. Both contributed to my economic fate.

When I maintained a success mindset throughout my days, everything else took care of itself. All good things follow mindset.

My mental practices compelled my daily actions, fueled my motivation, restored my strength, and attracted uncanny coincidences that harmonized with my financial goals.

Self-mastery is controlling our internal state regardless of external conditions. It is mental transcendence.

Keep your mind on wealth throughout every day—focus on being the successful person who already owns it.

When doubts or worries appear, focus on being a successful person.

You need to control your mind to focus on outcomes and become the power that grows acorns into oak trees. It's in you, this God Power.

The right actions spring from a focused mind.

The essence of self-mastery is the clarity to know exactly what we want, the discipline to carry our goals with us during our days, and the awareness to feel and be a successful person in advance of our crowning achievements.

It's not problems that cause our suffering, but an unprepared mind that allows the suffering. The person who expects daily challenges will not become overwhelmed. This is the first lesson.

Expand your mind until you no longer fit into your current environment. You will then witness that all gardens grow from the mind of the gardener.

On Mind

When the mind expands, the possibilities multiply. An inner wisdom will guide your ways if only you pause to listen to it.

I learned to focus my thoughts on what I wanted most, and then experience these outcomes in my imagination with an absurd faith.

I do believe we still have a lot to learn about the powers of the mind when it is charged up and focused on a single purpose.

> *Focus on the end, cling to your ideal outcome through thick and thin, and concentrate your attention.*

You must command your mind and set upon the building of your character. Like a sculptor with a rare vision, the seeker of wealth needs extraordinary resolve to achieve uncommon riches.

An unprepared mind invites suffering during the challenges of the day. But a battle-ready mind leads to poise in turbulent conditions.

I have seen coincidences that appear as miracles. And I believe these miracles are natural phenomena of a cause and effect that Nature has not yet revealed to us.

The rain in my life fell in the form of uncanny breaks, inspirations, coincidences, plans, and opportunities. My fortune was not all from my own hands. Then again, without the work of my own hands, my dreams would have surely been in vain.

I needed both hard work and lucky breaks.

Once a goal takes root in the mind and we gain faith surrounding its attainment, the world slowly changes—and coincidences show up.

Wealth requires hard work, but prosperity usually involves some lucky breaks. Only a superficial gardener takes all the credit, blind to the serendipity that harmonizes with one's aspirations.

We produce serendipity and synchronicity according to the depth of our faith.

It is always easy to discredit the uncanny events that show up in harmony with our ambitions. But Universal Intelligence operates through serendipity, and we can always chalk it up to coincidence.

We call it synchronicity or serendipity when life curiously unfolds in harmony with our thoughts of gratitude for the things we want.

Our problems are a call to use our greatest powers.

One hundred percent of your potential looks like an obsession. But it will awaken the Silent Power that exists in the garden and works behind the scenes to make the plants grow.

You are trapped by your lack of aim, and you'll always be trapped until you stop making excuses. You need to control your mind to focus on outcomes and become the power that grows acorns into oak trees. You have within your mind that potential of Universal Intelligence to shape your conditions.

I visualized patients calling the clinic, controlled my thoughts, radiated gratitude, and concentrated intensely on my goals. And I witnessed the phone ringing off the hook.

Wealth and Focus

If you can't narrow your focus, you'll forever dissipate your potential during the crowded days of an ordinary life.

I wanted to be the decider of my fate, never the one whose fate was decided by others. This was my focus for years during the climb.

With clarity of goals and focus on results, we can always improve our impact, and this should give us hope.

I sensed that my new focus and determination had caused a mysterious harmony with a Cooperative Energy. It seemed to connect me to an Intelligence that handed over ideas, plans, and lucky breaks.

The mental discipline of focusing on a goal sustains the attitude, fuels the determination, and perhaps even produces some lucky breaks in the accumulation of money.

Financial results came by harnessing my attention with a daily ritual of intense focus on outcomes. It was just deep concentration.

If I focused my attention on my goals every day, the proper attitude and actions filled up my hours.

> *I learned to focus on why I was doing the work, and not on the burden of doing it. Focus makes all the difference in the world.*

The key to enduring our hardest work is to focus on meaning.

I focused not on the drudgery, but on the hope that my family would benefit from my labor, struggle, fatigue, and sacrifices.

When self-pity descended on me, I focused on my why. I never forgot that I was engaged in this undertaking to win my financial freedom.

Decide exactly how much money you desire and why you want it, and focus on these things daily. We fail our potential if we can't focus our efforts with a schedule.

When all seems lost and there's no hope, we must focus with burning gratitude on a successful outcome. It's good to be a little crazy.

> *We're happier when we're busy and focused on getting something we want out of our days.*

It's our focus during the plowing that determines the day's suffering.

We are at our best when we are dialed in, turned on, focused deeply, lost in each passing moment.

When trapped in the struggles of the middle class, I found my best solutions during my focused think walks.

Wealth rewards a narrow focus on potent activities.

Cut the frivolous and mundane pursuits that waste time. Focus your power. Focus your energy. Focus your time.

It's vital to focus on one goal and track results, but stay flexible with your plans.

> *Focus on your desired outcome and wait for hunches, ideas, and thought flashes. Guidance comes in the form of sounder plans.*

The more you focus on solving a problem, the quicker you'll discover a solution.

Deliberate daily focus attracts ideas, people, situations, and events to support our goals.

Focus of daily hours is the equalizer of men.

Money comes to those who seek it and sacrifice their contradictory desires. It eludes those with scattered focus.

The days pass and, with focus, our wealth grows.

Those who get wealthy focus on their behaviors.

Start with a goal of prosperity—an exact amount of money—and give it a completion date. Then grow to be worthy of it. Expand your mind until you no longer fit into your current environment.

Set impossible goals, and then apply yourself to activities that impact the realization of those goals.

Productivity comes from following a plan, and a plan comes from a clear goal. It's knowing what you want and then staying the course.

The most productive hour of every day is the one you use to think about, imagine, dream, plan, and clarify your goals.

Concentrate on your desires and cultivate faith in your goals, but also give a sacred effort in the days to uphold your part of the bargain.

Realistic goals are for common lives, but wealthy are they who trust themselves to rise to the heights of their loftiest ambitions.

A realistic opinion is an argument for excuses that limit our goals and validate mediocre efforts.

Wealth favors the one whose decisions are influenced by clear goals and are visible in execution.

Mindful of my clear goals, I could always sense financial opportunity as well as the danger of inaction.

The average person with clear goals can outperform the most gifted person with no definite chief aim.

We leave our wealth to chance by failing to set financial goals.

Goals are to be trusted, not questioned.

Goals are not for the ordinary challenges of life; we only need a checklist for those things.

Goals are for extraordinary dreams we can't achieve from our current position. Goals invoke an inner wisdom we will never fully comprehend.

Goals open doors to unreasonable possibilities.

Goals clarify life, and they illuminate opportunities that are otherwise invisible.

Goals can even cause coincidences to show up according to your faith.

The only way to leave your income to chance is by failing to set a goal for it. Decide exactly how much money you desire and why you want it, and focus on these things daily.

On Mind

Goals lead to best actions and concentrated efforts.

Once a goal takes root in the mind and we gain faith surrounding its attainment, the world slowly changes—and coincidences show up.

Goals backed by faith led to the illumination of opportunities that were previously unnoticed.

If goals are magnets, then certitude is the magnetism.

Faith is the invisible force surrounding the goal we hold in mind that attracts the coincidences, cooperation, and lucky breaks.

Goal setting is easy, but goal getting requires strength.

Plans emerge from goals wrapped in faith.

We need to be fixed with our goals, open to feedback, always tracking results, and flexible with strategic plans.

Some people deride goal setting because they haven't yet built the mental muscle to regulate the mind to radiate absolute faith, all the time, day after day, as long as it takes to win.

When times are tough, we need a goal to stay on course. When times are good, we need a goal to keep the momentum.

Goals focus our thoughts, and our focus determines our plans.

On Mind

Goals center the inner wisdom that seeks to guide us.

Upward mobility relies on the daily capacity to hold a clear goal of wealth in the mind and to believe it will be achieved despite all evidence to the contrary.

Goal focus is the ultimate essence of self-mastery—and the battle of the mind is waged anew every day.

We may miss our goals due to external factors, but our daily thinking ensures our end victory.

Choosing our life direction is sometimes the only strategy that makes sense when our goals seem impossible. It's about staying the course.

To reach our potential, we must never cower from the bigger goals that are out of reach.

Goals are your future. Don't water them down. Make them big enough to scare you. Choose goals that make you uncomfortable.

If you will dare to dream and then endure with discipline the temporary discomforts, you will stand out among the masses.

Keep a vision of wealth close to your heart. Write goals and read them at night and in the morning.

Gardens don't respond to future intentions, and dreams don't respond to the actions of someday.

The power of intention is directing the energy of a human mind on things yet unseen in the physical world.

Our daily intention—the longings that dominate our waking hours—is the conductor of wealth affairs.

We control little more than daily intention, but that's more than enough because intention is the conductor of wealth.

Financial results came by harnessing my attention with a daily ritual of intense focus on outcomes. I didn't "kind of know what I wanted"—I knew my exact goals and wrote them repetitiously.

Urgent tasks get our attention, while important tasks get our resistance.

When we focus our attention on goals every day, the proper attitude and actions will fill up our hours, days, months, and years.

Our defining moments don't arrive with a trumpet blast to get our attention. When we don't decide, we erase all future possibilities.

Using your imagination, create images to give shape and form to thoughts and ideas. Draw them. And then give attention to these images as a repetitive mental practice.

We must trust the power of focused concentration. Attention and intention are the cure of hopelessness. Just give it your attention.

And somehow our attention on things invisible leads to their future realization.

Learn to focus your attention on the goals that you want to achieve and on finding ways to achieve those goals.

You will see your dreams take root if you do your part and water them with daily attention.

What gets measured certainly gets our attention. If you want financial accumulation, measure it. Keep a running tally.

The accumulation of money is the fruition of a strong purpose that endures despite the obstacles. What is your purpose for fortune?

A purpose for wealth, beyond hoarding it, is vital to sustain the ongoing persistence needed to acquire it.

My top reason to strive for prosperity and wealth was to be able to one day pursue more important purposes than making money.

Why do you want wealth? Your deeper cause fuels the persistence behind the sacrifices of financial achievement.

Focus on the end, cling to your ideal outcome through thick and thin, and concentrate your attention. This is your challenge.

A compelling purpose for wealth provides the drive you need to overcome the odds.

A big why is a deep purpose that drives sacrifice, a cause that fuels persistence. Our willpower is fueled by our why power.

Discipline will wane when the climbing gets steep, but a compelling purpose for the money fortifies your determination.

A deeper cause fuels the persistence behind the sacrifices of achievement. You need to develop a cause, a meaning, to keep you going through hard times.

Persistence is the expression of a compelling cause—a big why.

Great work endures due to great causes.

Wealth isn't easy. And there is no such thing as an easy life that contributes much to a worthy cause.

Drudgery can have meaning if it's done for a reason that advances you in some way. The key to enduring your hardest work is to focus on meaning. You must focus on why you are in this project.

Clarity of goals is at the heart of making better decisions.

Your definite chief aim is the mental clarity that precedes all strategic plans, key decisions, and subsequent actions.

So I must ask: Are you doing anything to gain clarity, or have you stopped thinking altogether? What is your exact goal, and why?

Wealth requires either willpower or why power, and the latter is often the real source of the former.

A big why pushes us, regardless of our mood, energy, state of mind, or even attitude.

I always wanted power over my affairs in life. This need for control drove me to urgently save money while others didn't seem to care as much about monetary accumulation.

It seems that average people think about money, want it, but stop thinking. Be the exception who clearly chooses to accumulate it.

Wealth and Faith

Our big goals need our faith before we know the way.

Absolute faith is knowing, in the face of overwhelming odds, and against a world that opposes you, that you absolutely will not fail!

I found that faith required daily vigilance of thought, but also learned that faith was the magnetic force surrounding my goals.

> *Feel prosperous until it feels natural. Drive wealth deep into your mind. Build a faith that displaces all doubts.*

You must develop a burning faith in the fulfillment of goals and aspirations by pretending and imagining that you have already achieved what you want most in terms of money.

If you can imagine this money with absolute faith that you will have it, and if you can maintain this mind-set for as long as it takes, then everything else will work out. You will find a way to earn it.

It requires persistence to develop faith in our financial goals.

Once a goal takes root in the mind and we gain faith surrounding its attainment, the world slowly changes—and coincidences show up.

What I know for sure is that a deep faith feels like gratitude. There's a calmness in real faith—a joy, a trust, a knowing.

The power of self-trust is integral to wealth because in life we get the poorest conditions we will tolerate.

You must always trust that you can achieve.

Self-trust is confidence in one's ability to achieve an objective.

If we think we can live the life of our dreams, we'll usually try.

Our self-trust determines the size of our goals, what we tolerate, and what we strive to attain. By contrast, self-doubt allows poor conditions. So we must build our faith if we want to be wealthy.

With the confidence to achieve, we trust ourselves to pay any price, handle any adversity, overcome mistakes, and occasionally reroute to a new end destination.

I saw that confidence conquers unwanted conditions, and self-trust influenced what I would not accept.

When we are too focused on the obstacles of wealth, it means we're not trusting the magical power of goals. We need to build our faith.

Goals are to be trusted, not questioned.

I was open-minded enough to trust that Universal Intelligence would notice if I stirred up a burning gratitude for an outcome.

With clarity and faith, the seeds of wealth will grow in the right seasons.

We only need to set a steady direction toward our aspirations and then trust the Universal Intelligence to assist our dreams according to our faith.

When things aren't going our way, worrying about money is dangerous. When all seems lost and there's no hope, we must focus with burning gratitude on a successful outcome.

> *When we are grateful in advance, we take our foot off the brake and move into a dimension of allowing good things to happen. It feels like success is the natural order of things—and it is.*

A burning gratitude for future triumph is the silent command that awakens a Sleeping Giant.

With gratitude, we trigger Universal Intelligence to help our cause.

With gratitude, we speak the language of Universal Intelligence and ask for an assist—even if our purpose is material wealth.

I used gratitude as a practice to build faith in full expectation of results, because I'd seen it work in my life—it wasn't a theory. And I would use every advantage, including the power of my mind, to get an optimal result.

Gratitude is an emotion that empowers our prayers.

Gratitude is the vibration of thought that seems to influence people, places, and events.

Gratitude is an Intangible Force. Things get arranged, it seems, in unfathomable ways. We call it synchronicity or serendipity when life curiously unfolds in harmony with our thoughts of gratitude.

It's beyond my power to explain serendipity. I can only attest to the fact that coincidences happen at a frequency so consistent that it makes me believe in a causal relationship when I do my part to discipline my mind in gratitude.

When I felt gratitude for future results, lucky breaks showed up. At times, these results were so immense that they scared me. I had to stop the daily practice of gratitude due to my fear of the results.

I learned to regulate my daily consciousness, and to live each moment with gratitude for wealth.

If gratitude opens the door of opportunity, then certitude kicks it down.

If gratitude is the state of mind that works in prayer, then certitude is the state of mind that works in battle.

Gratitude is faith during peace; certitude is faith during war.

> *Certitude is knowing, not believing. It is undiluted faith, a supreme form of consciousness that transcends reality and, at its height of empowerment, imposes its authority. In this state, the odds don't matter.*

Certitude is an angry stubbornness that won't be denied; it is a certainty, an inevitability of outcome, no matter what. It is a nonnegotiable idea, a foregone conclusion in the mind.

Our gratitude sets events in motion, but our certitude wins the battles during the days.

An attitude of certitude—tenacious mindfulness that influences people, places, and events—is a common trait of goal achievers.

If goals are magnets, then certitude is the magnetism. It's the invisible force surrounding the goal we hold in mind that attracts the coincidences, cooperation, and lucky breaks.

Wealth and Intuition

When we ignore our inner wisdom, we will come to regret it.

We don't always get to see the end when we choose our direction. Sometimes a feeling is all we will have to guide us on the way.

We all have a sixth sense—our inner wisdom—that exists in stillness and silence. And if we pause, we can access this guidance.

> *We all have instincts that can guide us if only we pay attention to them.*

I made better choices for upward mobility by paying attention when something felt wrong.

In stillness I sensed that this direction was right, and I trusted this sense. And that is exactly the essence of following our emotional guidance system—it leads us by an inner pull that won't die.

Goals invoke an inner wisdom we will never fully comprehend. Goals open doors to unreasonable possibilities.

On Mind

Our inner wisdom emerges from our inner vision.

If we are mindful to pause for a few seconds, we can consult an inner wisdom that is available to those who seek it.

Over the years, I have learned to consult my inner wisdom for an internal "red light" or "green light." A red light just feels like something's wrong. A green light is the absence of a red light.

Goals also center the inner wisdom that seeks to guide us.

Control your mind, and then let your inner wisdom direct you.

We may have an inner wisdom, but we are free to ignore it.

Life is difficult alone. Stay close to the Source. Be aware of silent promptings. Direct your thoughts; heed your inner wisdom.

We each have a right path, and we all have an inner voice. When a dream persists in the heart and has staying power over many years, I view the attraction with a sacred veneration.

It seems that the inner voice resonates with something deep within the Universal Intelligence that governs this world.

Our authentic pull of the inner voice is a persistent aspiration that won't die. It lasts the test of time.

On Mind

Our greatest regrets arise from missed opportunities to live an authentic life aligned with our individuality. And these regrets arise from ignoring the inner voice.

My inner voice feels like either a silent pull toward or a strong repulsion away from a person, choice, or direction.

The inner voice influences our direction before we can see the map. And the road always leads us directly into great uncertainties.

The inner voice is waiting to guide us if only we ask good questions and stay attuned to our feelings during our days. What will you regret if you don't do it, see it, or try it? The answer, when it comes, and, most important, when it stays, is commonly the inner voice.

It may be the inner voice speaking loudly when we feel boredom, worry, doubt, frustration, a sense of being overwhelmed, despair, financial insecurity, and hopelessness.

It's always best to avoid financial setbacks, and run when something doesn't feel right. Warnings exist in feelings of discord for those who pause and listen to their intuition.

Only a fool ignores their intuition.

When you sense a bad feeling about a direction, don't dismiss it as a trivial detail.

I've never seen good things happen when one ignores a troubled sixth sense.

We can sense future calamity if we simply pause during our hectic days and listen to our intuition.

When we use both our reason and our intuition, it's possible to avoid all financial disasters. And the key word is, ALL.

We all have a sixth sense—our inner wisdom—that exists in stillness and silence. And if we pause, we can access this guidance.

When a change is needed, we know it through a sixth sense.
A sixth sense is a feeling of resonance or discord after weighing the known facts.

Our sixth sense can warn us of impending dangers and help us avoid future financial setback.

I made better choices for upward mobility by paying attention when something felt wrong.

There's guidance for our actions in the stillness. But sometimes a feeling is all we will have to guide us on the way.

Use your hearts, minds, and ability to choose. Never disregard the guidance of emotions. Stay close to the Source of your feelings. Be mindful to pause and listen every day for inner wisdom.

We all have instincts that will guide us if only we pay attention to them.

You'll find that guidance comes to you in the form of sounder plans.

You'll be guided if only you "remember to remember" to pause and listen to your own inner voice.

Over the years, I have learned to consult my inner wisdom for an internal "red light" or "green light." It's the subtle feeling of resonance with a decision—a mild discord or an inner peace surrounding a choice. It's a gut hunch, a deep instinct, a sense that something feels right or wrong.

Wealth and Thinking

Always distrust your thinking under exhaustion. Not all thinking leads to good things. Your past thinking caused all your current troubles.

An emotional mind makes mistakes, while a rational mind makes money. Let passion give way to reason when dreaming gives way to planning. The enemy of wealth building is an impulsive decision.

Wealth requires strategic thinking with a calm respect for the worst consequences. Those without prudence often learn the pain of misjudgments.

It is always in one's best interest to pause long, think calmly, and consider the worst-case scenarios before making a decision.

Thinking is work; it is doing something. It's a vital action. And the wealthy tend to think more about wealth and then prioritize it.

Clear thinking is a learned skill, and since thinking directs the days of work, it the single most impactful use of our free time.

Thinking of wealth leads to behaviors that lead to accumulation.

Regardless of the causes behind it, what we think about tends to become our reality. The outer world is but a reflection of our inner world. This isn't esoteric ballyhoo. It's visible and observable.

The wealthy think of accumulation. They are wired to think differently.

> *The wealthy think about wealth. They have goals. They spend time alone in reflection. They study and read about wealth. They study and plan ways to grow richer. They know how much they are worth, how much they earn, how much they spend, and where the money goes. The wealthy are happier due to their security, options, and success. They are competent at money. And they are always trying to gain more profits by increasing their earnings while decreasing their expenses.*

The wealthy think about money more seriously. They sacrifice the luxuries of today for the promise of tomorrow due to their vision.

You must not think of yourself as too good for any task, nor think that you're entitled to free time, entertainment, comforts, status symbols, or showy extravagance. Instant gratification prevents wealth.

Our conditions today can be traced to our past choices and actions.

You are in charge, at least at the time of a decision, before your choices and conditions gain the upper hand and then control you.

On Mind

Your life will be the result of choices, and the best decisions result from deeper knowledge. Spend time to think as you choose.

I faced daily choices between spending or saving, and gained upward mobility through sacrifice and modesty.

> *Clarity of goals is at the heart of making better decisions. The presence of a target, a financial objective, provides the essential criteria by which we can judge the consequences of our many decisions. Should we buy the luxury car? What are our savings goals? Should we accept the new job or go back to school? What are our income goals? Should we exercise or relax? What are our health goals? Should we take an expensive vacation or save for retirement? What kind of life do we want when we're older?*

We need to periodically get out of the whirlwind to think about the whirlwind. We must get out of the frame to repaint the picture.

Seek uncompressed time to get in tune with your inner wisdom, and to reevaluate your direction. Reflect on what you want most in life, and why you want it. Get away to eliminate the distractions of life.

Broad-stroke, big-picture, macro-view thinking is most possible in the uncompressed time of periodic retreats. It can be just a weekend spent reviewing goals or an entire week getting away from it all.

We need to periodically get out of the whirlwind to think about the whirlwind. We must get out of the frame to see the picture.

I saw that the best plans unfolded in uncompressed times, and so I went on retreats to contemplate my life.

Your discontentment is good and beneficial. It keeps you stirred up so that you use your time. And it can fuel you to do great things.

I learned to distrust my thinking under exhaustion, and to build my strength to operate in my best state of maximum energy and power.

Reflect on what you want most in life, and why you want it. When you like your direction, think about how to improve things with increased effectiveness. Think about your life to avoid future regrets.

We should practice thinking alone daily. In addition, there's just something about getting away and taking a retreat. We should periodically get out of the whirlwind to allow the mind to relax, expand, and soar. We can think best on a retreat.

When he stayed with a problem long enough, giving it time in his days, leaning into the issue with focused contemplation, the solution always came to mind. Problems are a call to use our greatest powers.

Enlightened thinking happens if only we make time to think, and then focus the mind on a centering question. Make a list of ideas. If you are not creating a list of ideas, you're not thinking.

Walking gives us time alone, removes us from the whirlwind of our day and any interruptions, and provides a sanctuary from chaos where the mind can soar to greater heights.

On Mind

While walking may not be crucial to thinking, it provides time and space from the whirlwind of life and its distractions.

A solitary walk creates a rhythm of movement that synchronizes the body, mind, and spirit. It provides the time to ponder, evaluate, and strategize our lives. A walk can lead us to make better choices.

By thinking, *How can I. . . ?* we get out of the whirlwind. We become inventors of solutions. We become creative strategists who dig for practical plans. We become more resourceful thinkers.

The method of thinking How can I . . . ? forces the solutions.

> *We always get what we think about, but we get it more assuredly if we demand solutions and maintain goals backed by faith. We can come up with the most creative solutions by asking, How can I . . . ? This is an essential question for wealth.*

Upward mobility demands accurate thinking, and often our best thinking will happen on mindful walks. A body in motion gets the mind in motion—and out of the commotion.

The poor stay poor for many reasons, but the two factors most under their control are their daily behaviors and daily thinking.

I never face a major life decision, adopt a new strategy, or try to solve a problem without first mulling it over on a think walk.

Admittedly, there is no doubt that people can think and solve problems just fine without walks. Our mental faculties obviously work when we are sitting in a chair, pacing in an office, or driving a car. But walking creates moments of isolation, and in this age of distraction, a walk can be a ritual to remove us from the buzz.

While walking may not be crucial to thinking, it provides time and space from the whirlwind of life and its distractions.

A walk creates a rhythm of movement that synchronizes the body, mind, and spirit. It provides the time to ponder, evaluate, and strategize our lives.

When trapped in the struggles of the middle class, I found my best solutions during my focused think walks.

Internal thinking—not external forces—causes most failures.

We may miss our goals due to external factors, but our daily thinking ensures our end victory.

Thinking big is vital to gain our best life. Will you willingly choose to walk into unfamiliar places to get to your cherished dreams?

If your life is perfect, then you get a pass. But if you need a boost, if you feel inadequate to meet your challenges, if you feel doubtful of your ability to endure, you must exercise to unlock your full powers.

Exercise dramatically affects thinking. If we exercise, our days in the world will be better because we will be better in the world.

On Mind

We're not stuck with any limiting belief. We can change what we've always believed. It is wise to choose beliefs that empower wealth.

We each choose, or neglect to choose, our own destiny.

Think hard about the things you fear! We all have something to fear, but only the strongest will choose to face everything and rise.

We must forever choose ambition over comfort, effort over ease, exertions over excuses, and contribution over complacency.

Choose the path of most resistance. Do the dreadful things first every day, without exception! Do what you resist.

Choose goals that make you uncomfortable.

We must choose the hard life to earn our comforts.

Behind the defining moments of our lives, we will surely look back at a decision when we once took a risk and walked directly into uncertainty.

A decision without action is a delusion. When we don't decide, we erase all future possibilities.

There is no destiny. There is only decision.

Wealth favors the one whose decisions are influenced by clear goals and are visible in execution.

Our defining moments don't arrive with a trumpet blast to get our attention. When we don't decide, we erase all future possibilities.

In our lives, we are what we are, we have what we have, and we do what we do because of our past decisions.

A decision is a resolution defined by its action.

The cost of complacency is lost opportunity; our indecision erases many future possibilities.

I never face a major life decision, adopt a new strategy, or try to solve a problem without first mulling it over on a think walk.

It is always in one's best interest to pause long, think calmly, and consider the worst-case scenarios before making a decision.

You can decide not to try. You can try and fail. Or you can try and succeed. The only question is, upon your final breath, how will you feel about yourself having not tried?

PART IV: ON LESSONS

Time

Don't judge each day by the harvest you reap, but by the seeds that
you plant.   —Robert Louis Stevenson

Today is a king in disguise. Let us not be deceived, let us unmask the
king as he passes.   —Ralph Waldo Emerson

Don't say you don't have enough time. You have exactly the same
number of hours per day that were given to Helen Keller, Pasteur,
Michelangelo, Mother Teresa, Leonardo da Vinci, Thomas Jefferson,
and Albert Einstein.   —H. Jackson Brown Jr.

The value of life lies not in the length of days "but in the use we make
of them. A man may live long, but get very little.
                                                      —Michel de Montaigne

Time management is the sun, and everything that you do is the
planets in orbit.   — Brian Tracy

Dost thou love life? Then do not squander time, for that's the stuff
life is made of.   — Benjamin Franklin

Impact

Gardens are not made by singing "Oh, how beautiful," and sitting in
the shade.   —Rudyard Kipling

If we're unhappy with the harvest we're reaping, we should sow
different seed.   —Phil Pringle

Doing the right thing is more important than doing the thing right.
                                                   —Peter Drucker

All the flowers of tomorrow are in the seeds of today.   —Proverb

Financial Dignity

A garden gives the body the dignity of working in its own support. It
is a way of rejoining the human race.   —Wendell Berry

Poverty is uncomfortable, but nine times out of ten the best thing
that can happen to a young man is to be tossed overboard and
compelled to sink or swim.   —James Garfield

Do what you can, with what you've got, where you are.
                                                   —Theodore Roosevelt.

Work is the best friend I've ever known. It has brought me all the
good things I've had.   —George Clason

Mental Practices

The garden suggests there might be a place where we can meet
nature halfway.   —Michael Pollan

God gives every bird its food, but He does not throw it into its nest.
                                        —Josiah Gilbert Hollan

While calling on the gods a man should himself lend a hand.
                                        —Hippocrates

According to your faith, so shall it be done unto you.   —Jesus

Challenges

A good garden may have some weeds.   —Thomas Fuller

Difficulties are meant to rouse, not discourage. The human spirit is to
grow strong by conflict.   —William Ellery Channing

A smooth sea never made a skillful mariner.   —English Proverb

Do not pray for easy lives. Pray to be stronger men! Do not pray for
tasks equal to your powers. Pray for powers equal to your tasks.
                                        —Reverend Phillips Brooks

Do not pray for lighter burdens but for stronger backs.
                                        —Theodore Roosevelt

Crisis

A garden is always a series of losses set against a few triumphs, like
life itself.   —May Sarton

The first and final thing you have to do in this world is last in it and
not be smashed by it.   —Ernest Hemingway

Misfortune comes to all men.   —Chinese Proverb.

Endure, and preserve yourselves for better things.   —Virgil

I bend, but I do not break.   —Jean de la Fontaine

If you want to see the sunshine, you have to weather the storm.
                                                    —Frank Lane

In the depths of winter, I finally learned that within me there lay an
invincible summer.   —Albert Camus

Procrastination

A man of words and not of deeds is like a garden full of weeds.
                                            —English nursery rhyme

Somebody should tell us, right at the start of our lives, that we are
dying. Then we might live life to the limit, every minute of every day.
Do it! I say. Whatever you want to do, do it now! There are only so
many tomorrows.   —Pope Paul VI

Intangible Forces

The garden is a love song, a duet between a human being and
Mother Nature.   —Jeff Cox

Life always whispers to you first, but if you ignore the whisper,
sooner or later you'll get a scream.   —Oprah Winfrey

Wealth Seasons

A garden is where you can find a whole spectrum of life, birth and
death.   —Tiffany Baker

Look deep into nature, and then you will understand everything
better.   —Albert Einstein

April hath put a spirit of youth in everything.   —Shakespeare

Look, here is a tree in the garden and every summer it produces
apples, and we call it an apple tree because the tree 'apples.' That's
what it does.   —Alan Watts

There is a harmony in autumn, and a lustre in its sky which through
the summer is not heard or seen.   —Percy Bysshe Shelley

Adopt the pace of nature, her secret is patience.   —Emerson

Nature does not hurry, yet everything is accomplished.   —Lao Tzu

Purpose

I like gardening—it's a place where I find myself when I need to lose
myself.   —Alice Sebold

Life becomes harder for us when we live for others, but it also
becomes richer and happier.   —Albert Schweitzer

Compensation

My green thumb came only as a result of the mistakes made while
learning to see things from the plant's point of view.   —H. Fred Dale

Money is a headache, and money is the cure.   —Terri Guillemets

Never complain about your troubles; they are responsible for more
than half of your income.   —Robert R. Updegraff

One thing I do know for sure is that your rewards in life will be in
exact proportion to your human services. If you want more rewards,
you'd better throw more logs on the fire in the form of more service.
                                             —Earl Nightingale

We each serve a portion of humanity—our inner contacts, family,
friends, neighbors, coworkers, customers, prospects, and employers.
Wishing for more tangible or intangible rewards without giving more
or better service to others leads to frustrations, failure,
demoralization, and surrender."   —Earl Nightingale

Five-Year Crusades

There is no spot of ground, however arid, bare or ugly, that cannot be tamed into such a state as may give an impression of beauty and delight.   —Gertrude Jekyll

When patterns are broken, new worlds emerge.   —Tuli Kupferberg

Most people overestimate what they can do in one year, and underestimate what they can do in ten years.   —Bill Gates

Nothing worthwhile comes easily. Half Effort does not produce half results. It produces no results. Work, continuous work and hard work, is the only way to accomplish results that last. —Hamilton Holt

Continuous effort—not strength or intelligence—is the key to unlocking our potential.   —Winston Churchill

Every worthwhile accomplishment, big or little, has its stages of drudgery and triumph: a beginning, a struggle, and a victory.
                                            —Mahatma Gandhi

Resistance

Successful gardening is doing what has to be done when it has to be done the way it ought to be done whether you want to do it or not.
                                            —Jerry Baker

Any idiot can face a crisis; it's that everyday living that's rough.

On Lessons

—Clifford Odets

Rule of thumb: The more important a call or action is to our soul's evolution, the more Resistance we will feel toward pursuing it.

—Steven Pressfield

The distance is nothing; it is only the first step that is difficult.

—Marie de Vichy-Chamrond, Marquise du Deffand

Make it a point to do something every day that you don't want to do. This is the golden rule for acquiring the habit of doing your duty without pain.   —Mark Twain

A professional is someone who can do his best work when he doesn't feel like it.   —Alistair Cooke

If you have to eat two frogs, eat the ugliest one first.   —Brian Tracy

Productivity

The best fertilizer is the gardener's shadow.   —Anonymous

An earnest purpose finds time, or makes it. It seizes on spare moments, and turns fragments to golden account.

—William Ellery Channing

Much may be done in those little shreds and patches of time which every day produces, and which most men throw away.

—Charles Caleb Colton

Guard well your spare moments. They are like uncut diamonds. Discard them and their value will never be known. Improve them and they will become the brightest gems in a useful life.   —Emerson

Peak State

Early to bed, early to rise. Work like hell and fertilize.

—Emily Whaley

I go for a face sweat, as a minimum daily workout.   —Steve Young

I believe that when the body is strong, the mind thinks strong thoughts.   —Henry Rollins

It is exercise alone that supports the spirits, and keeps the mind in vigor.   —Cicero

A good sweat, with the blood pounding through my body, makes me feel alive, revitalized. I gain a sense of mastery and assurance. I feel good about myself.   —Arthur Dobrin

Sweat cleanses from the inside. It comes from places a shower will never reach.   —George A. Sheehan

To keep the body in good health is a duty—otherwise we shall not be able to keep our mind strong and clear.   —Buddha

Self-Trust

An optimistic gardener is one who believes that whatever goes down must come up.   —Leslie Hal

Self-trust is the first secret of success.   —Emerson

Argue for your limitations, and sure enough they're yours.
                                                    —Richard Bach

Self-confidence is the first requisite to great undertakings.
                                                    —Samuel Johnson

They are able because they think they are able.   —Virgil

He who has lost confidence can lose nothing more.
                                    —Pierre-Claude-Victor Boiste

It's not what you are that holds you back. It's what you think you are not.   —Denis Waitley

Low self-confidence isn't a life sentence. Self-confidence can be learned, practiced, and mastered—just like any other skill. Once you master it, everything in your life will change for the better.
                                                    —Barrie Davenport

It is not the mountain we conquer but ourselves.
                                                    —Sir Edmund Hillary

There must always be a burn in your heart to achieve. In the quiet of your solitude, close your eyes, bow your head, grit your teeth, clench

your fists. Achieve in your heart, vow and dedicate yourself to
achieve, to achieve.   —Trammell Crow

The will to do springs from the knowledge that we can do.
                                                    —William James

Convictions

Weeds are pulled up by the roots to clear the fields for the growing
grain. Why should not mental weeds be pulled up by the roots also,
and the mind cleared for growth?   —Horace Fletcher

Man is belief expressed.   —Phineas Quimby

Fulfilling Work

No two gardens are the same. No two days are the same in one
garden.   —Hugh Johnson

Learn what you are and be such.   —Pindar

The destiny of a man is in his own soul.   —Herodotus

Ninety percent of the world's woe comes from people not knowing
themselves, their abilities, their frailties, and even their real virtues.
                                                —Sydney J. Harris

Be true to one's self, follow not every impulse, but find out who one is. Discover a combination of interests and powers, and find through experiment and thought the course of life to fulfill those interests and powers most completely.   —Earl Nightingale

Inner Values

Can plants be happy? If they get what they need, they thrive—that's what I know.   —Terri Guillemets

The way you live your life provides clues, such as how you spend your time and money.   —Sidney B. Simon

Choice of aim is clearly a matter of clarification of values, especially on the choice between possible options.   —W. Edwards Deming

Success in the knowledge economy comes to those who know themselves, their strengths, their values, and how they best perform.
—Peter Drucker

Inclinations

What is a weed? A plant whose virtues have not yet been discovered.
—Ralph Waldo Emerson

When you put your preferences on the altar of your life and say: THIS. THIS is what compels me. The real you emerges.
—Danielle LaPorte

How can we explain such inclinations? They are forces within us . . . draw[ing] us to certain experiences and away from others. As these forces move us here or there, they influence the development of our minds in very particular ways . . . If you allow yourself to learn who you really are by paying attention to that voice and force within you, then you can become what you were fated to become—an individual, a Master. —Robert Greene

There is a vast world of work out there in this country, where at least 111 million people are employed in this country alone—many of whom are bored out of their minds. All day long. —Richard Nelson Bolles

If passion drives, let reason hold the reins. —Benjamin Franklin

You begin by choosing a field or position that roughly corresponds to your inclinations. This initial position offers you room to maneuver and important skills to learn . . . You adjust and perhaps move to a related field, continuing to learn more about yourself, but always expanding off your skill base . . . Eventually, you will hit upon a particular field, niche, or opportunity that suits you perfectly. You will recognize it when you find it because it will spark that childlike sense of wonder and excitement; it will feel right. —Robert Greene

A man can succeed at almost anything for which he has unlimited enthusiasm. —Charles Schwab

Knacks

Talent is like a flower. You have to fully tend to it if you want
something beautiful.   —Marinela Reka

Nature arms each man with some faculty which enables him to do
easily some feat impossible to any other. —Ralph Waldo Emerson

A winner is someone who recognizes his God-given talents, works his
tail off to develop them into skills, and uses these skills to accomplish
his goals.   —Larry Bird

If only every man would make proper use of his strength and do his
utmost, he need never regret his limited ability.   —Cicero

Skills vary with the man. We must . . . strive by that which is born in
us.   —Pindar

In my clinical experience, the greatest block to a person's
development is his having to take on a way of life which is not rooted
in his own powers.   —Rollo May

Ambition

Gardening is a kind of disease. It infects you, you cannot escape it.
                                            —Lewis Gannett

A man's worth is no greater than his ambitions.   —Marcus Aurelius

Not failure, but low aim, is crime.   —Ernest Holmes

A man without ambition is a bird without wings.
                                        —Walter H. Cottingham

I am thankful to God for all the blessings in my life. But I am also thankful for the ambition I was given to earn these many blessings in my life.   – Bud Soforic

People who are unable to motivate themselves must be content with mediocrity, no matter how impressive their other talents.
                                        —Andrew Carnegie

The artist is nothing without the gift, but the gift is nothing without work.   —Émile Zola

Inner Voice

I have never had so many good ideas day after day as when I worked in the garden.   —John Erskine

Sometimes the heart sees what is invisible to the eye.
                                        —H. Jackson Brown Jr.

First and foremost, think straight, trust the quiet inner voice that tells you what to do.   —Wilhelm Reich

We all have an inner teacher, an inner guide, an inner voice that speaks very clearly but usually not very loudly. That information can be drowned out by the chatter of the mind and the pressure of day-to-day events. But if we quiet down the mind, we can begin to hear what we're not paying attention to. We can find out what's right for us.   —Dean Ornish

Courage

The mighty oak was once a little nut that stood its ground.

—Unknown

I knew that if I failed, I wouldn't regret that. But I knew the one thing I might regret is not trying.   —Jeff Bezos

It is hard to fail, but it is worse never to have tried to succeed.

—Theodore Roosevelt

Be Unrealistic

Gardening is a way of showing that you believe in tomorrow.

—Unknown

Once the 'what' is decided, the 'how' always follows. We must not make the 'how' an excuse for not facing and accepting the 'what.'

—Pearl S. Buck

The way to see by faith, is to shut the Eye of Reason.

—Benjamin Franklin.

Faith that the thing can be done is essential to any great
achievement.   —Thomas N. Carruthers

I have learned to use the word 'impossible,' with the greatest
caution.   —Wernher von Braun

Being realistic is the most commonly traveled road to mediocrity.
                                                            —Will Smith

Fortitude

Farming looks mighty easy when your plow is a pencil, and you're a
thousand miles from the cornfield. -   —Dwight D. Eisenhower

Genius begins great works; labor alone finished them.
                                                            —Joseph Joubert

You will never succeed beyond the purpose to which you are willing
to surrender. And your surrender will not be complete until you have
formed the habit of doing the things that failures don't like to do.
                                                            —Albert E. N. Gray

Inner Circle

Friends are the flowers in the garden of life.   —Mary Engelbreit

He that walketh with wise men shall be wise.   —Proverbs 13:20

On Lessons

Every man is like the company he is wont to keep.   —Euripides

Have no friends not equal to yourself.   —Confucius

Be courteous to all, but intimate with few, and let those few be well tried before you give them your confidence.

—George Washington

Decision

What I've always found interesting in gardens is looking at what people choose to plant there. What they put in. What they leave out. One small choice and then another, and soon there is a mood, an atmosphere, a series of limitations, a world. —Helen Humphrey

We are all self-made, but only the successful will admit it.

—Earl Nightingale

It is in your moments of decision that your destiny is shaped.

—Tony Robbins

Sacred Efforts

Gardening is the work of a lifetime: you never finish.

—Oscar de La Renta

Satisfaction lies in the effort, not in the attainment. Full effort is full victory.   —Mahatma Gandhi

I am seeking, I am striving, I am in it with all my heart.

—Vincent van Gogh

Do not look for approval except for the consciousness of doing your best.　　　　　　　　　　　　　　　　　　—Andrew Carnegie

To have striven, to have made an effort, to have been true to certain ideals—this alone is worth the struggle.　　　　　　—William Osler

It is by spending oneself that one becomes rich.　　—Sarah Bernhardt

Money Goals

We learn from our gardens to deal with the most urgent question of the time: How much is enough?　　　　　　　　　—Wendell Berry

Money is better than poverty, if only for financial reasons.

—Woody Allen

The victory of success is half won when one gains the habit of setting goals and achieving them.　　　　　　　　　　—Og Mandino

An average person with average talent, ambition and education can outstrip the most brilliant genius in our society, if that person has clear, focused goals.　　　　　　　　　　　　　　—Brian Tracy

Schedule

A day is Eternity's seed, and we are its Gardeners. —Erika Harris

The highest value in life is found in the stewardship of time.
—Robert M. Fine

To live the greatest number of good hours is wisdom.
—Ralph Waldo Emerson

Wasted time means wasted lives. —Robert R. Shannon

Our potential is one thing. What we do with it is quite another.
—Angela Duckworth

Lack of direction, not lack of time, is the problem. —Zig Ziglar

We all have twenty-four hours a day. A man who dares to waste one hour of time has not discovered the value of life.
—Charles Darwin

Big Why

Gardening is a matter of your enthusiasm holding up until your back gets used to it. —Anonymous

Great minds have purposes, others have wishes.
—Washington Irving

The more I want to get something done, the less I call it work.

On Lessons

—Richard Bach

Continuity of purpose is one of the most essential ingredients of happiness in the long run, and for most men this comes chiefly through their work. —Bertrand Russell

Nothing can resist a will which will stake even existence on its fulfillment. —Benjamin Disraeli

If you really want to do something, you'll find a way. If you don't, you'll find an excuse. —Jim Rohn

Always bear in mind that your own resolution to succeed is more important than any other one thing. —Abraham Lincoln

He who has a why to live, can bear almost any how.
—Friedrich Nietzsche

Gratitude

In all things of Nature there is something of the marvelous.
—Aristotle

Prayers not felt by us are seldom heard by God. —Philip Henry

We give thanks for unknown blessings already on their way.
—Sacred chant of ancient ritual.

Whatever things you desire, when you pray, believe that you receive them, and you shall have them. —Jesus

Certitude

A garden is a grand teacher. It teaches patience and careful
watchfulness; it teaches industry and thrift; above all it teaches
entire trust.   —Gertrude Jekyll

Goals are like magnets. They'll attract the things that make them
come true.   —Tony Robbins

They've got us surrounded again, the poor bastards!
                                    — General Creighton Abrams Jr.

Intention

Your mind is a garden. Your thoughts are the seeds. You can grow
flowers or you can grow weeds. -   —Anonymous

Vision is the art of seeing things invisible.   —Jonathan Swift

All things are created twice. There's a mental or first creation, and a
physical or second creation, to all things.   —Stephen R. Covey

Everything is created twice, first in the mind and then in reality.
                                                       —Robin Sharma

You can only see one thing clearly, and that is your goal. Form a
mental vision of that and cling to it through thick and thin.
                                                       —Kathleen Norris.

Dream lofty dreams, and as you dream, so shall you become. Your vision is the promise of what you shall . . . at last unveil.

—James Allen

Meditation

There is always Music amongst the trees in the Garden, but our hearts must be very quiet to hear it.   —Minnie Aumonier

Your phone has a charger, right?. It's like having a charger for your whole body and mind. That's what [transcendental] meditation is!

—Jerry Seinfeld

Prayer does not change God, but it changes him who prays.

—Søren Kierkegaard

Meditation is a mental discipline that enables us to do one thing at a time.   —Max Picard

When you focus on repeating that mantra over and over again, soon the noise will die down and all you will hear is your inner voice.

—Russell Simmons

If you just sit and observe, you will see how restless your mind is. If you try to calm it, it only makes it worse, but over time it does calm, and when it does, there's room to hear more subtle things—that's when your intuition starts to blossom and you start to see things more clearly and be in the present more. Your mind just slows down, and you see a tremendous expanse in the moment. You see so much more than you could see before.   —Steve Jobs

I think meditation has been the single biggest reason for whatever success I've had . . . I can be stressed, or tired, and I can go into meditation and it all just flows out of me. I'll come out refreshed and centered . . . Meditation helps you stay in a calm, clear-headed state so that when challenges come at you, you can deal with them like a ninja—in a calm thoughtful way. When you're centered, your emotions are not hijacking you.   —Ray Dalio

Meditation is not a way of making your mind quiet. It is a way of entering into the quiet that is already there—buried under the fifty thousand thoughts the average person thinks every day.

—Deepak Chopra

Mindfulness

In order to live off a garden, you practically have to live in it.

—Kin Hubbard

A man's life is what his thoughts make of it.   —Marcus Aurelius

A man is literally what he thinks.   —James Allen

A man is what he thinks about all day long.   —Ralph Waldo Emerson

Mindfulness isn't difficult. We just need to remember to do it.

—Sharon Salzberg

If you want to hit a bird on the wing, you must have all your will in focus, you must not be thinking about yourself and, equally, you must not be thinking about your neighbor: you must be living in your eye on that bird. Every achievement is a bird on the wing.

—Oliver Wendell Holmes Jr.

"There is a voice inside of you
That whispers all day long,
"I feel that this is right for me,
I know that this is wrong."
No teacher, preacher, parent, friend
Or wise man can decide
What's right for you—just listen to
The voice that speaks inside.

—Shel Silverstein

Retreat

My spirit was lifted and my soul nourished by my time in the garden. It gave me a calm connection with all of life, and an awareness that remains with me now, long after leaving the garden.

—Nancy Ross Hugo

To do much clear thinking, a person must arrange for regular periods of solitude when they can concentrate and indulge the imagination without distraction. —Thomas Edison

Most people spend their whole lives climbing the ladder of success, only to realize when they get to the top, the ladder was leaning against the wrong wall. —Stephen R. Covey

Sixth Sense

Let us give Nature a chance; she knows her business better than we
do.   —Michel de Montaigne

Trust your hunches. They're usually based on facts filed away just
below the conscious level.   —Dr. Joyce Brothers

Every time I've done something that doesn't feel right, it's ended up
not being right.   —Mario Cuomo

If it doesn't feel right, don't do it. That is the lesson, and that lesson
alone will save you a lot of grief.   —Oprah Winfrey

To make the right choices in life, you have to get in touch with your
soul. To do this, you need to experience solitude . . . because in the
silence you hear the truth and know the solutions.

—Deepak Chopra

Discontentment

Without hard work, nothing grows but weeds.   —Gordon B. Hinckle

We're at our best and our happiest when we're fully engaged,
climbing, thinking, planning, working—when we're on the road to
something we want very much.   —Earl Nightingale

From the discontent of man, the world's best progress springs.

—Ella Wheeler

Restlessness is discontent, and discontent is the first necessity of
progress.   Thomas Edison

People wish to be settled; only as far as they are unsettled is there
any hope for them.   Ralph Waldo Emerson

Financial Fear

One of the worst mistakes you can make as a gardener is to think
you're in charge.   —Janet Gillespie

Fear is a good thing. It means you're paying attention.
                                                   —Tamora Pierce

Feeling fear is a good sign that your survival instincts are intact. You
need to appreciate the dangers to stay safe.   —Zoe Bell

Straight Edge

Gardening is a kind of disease . . . You interrupt the serious cocktail
drinking because of an irresistible impulse to get up and pull a weed.
                                                   —Lewis Gannett

I can't stand anything that clouds my mind. I have no problem with
people drinking; I have no problem with other people smoking dope.
If that's what they want to do, God bless them, that's their business.
But I can't do those things.   —Larry Ellison

I have better use for my brain than to poison it with alcohol. To put alcohol in a human brain is like putting sand in the bearings of an engine.   —Thomas Edison

The two biggest weak links in my experience, are liquor and leverage.
                                          —Warren Buffett

Sobriety is the strength of the soul, for it preserves its reason unclouded by passion.   —Pythagoras

I made a commitment to completely cut out drinking and anything that might hamper me from getting my mind and body together. And the floodgates of goodness have opened upon me—spiritually and financially.   —Denzel Washington

Discomfort Bridges

Why not go out on a limb? Isn't that where the fruit is?
                                          —Frank Scullyn

Imagine that in order to have a great life you have to cross a dangerous jungle. You can stay safe where you are and have an ordinary life, or you can risk crossing the jungle to have a terrific life. How would you approach that choice? Take a moment to think about it because it is the sort of choice that, in one form or another, we all have to make.   —Ray Dalio

The quality of your life is directly related to how much uncertainty you can comfortably handle. What you are afraid to do is a clear indication of the next thing you need to do.   —Tony Robbins

He has not learned the lesson of life who does not every day
surmount a fear.   —Ralph Waldo Emerson

If we are not a little bit uncomfortable every day, we're not growing.
All the good stuff is outside our comfort zone.   —Jack Canfield

Nobody ever died of discomfort, yet living in the name of comfort has
killed more ideas, more opportunities, more actions, and more
growth than everything else combined. Comfort kills!
                                                —T. Harv Eker

Don't let the fear of the time it will take to accomplish something
stand in the way of your doing it. The time will pass anyway; we
might just as well put that passing time to the best possible use.
                                                —Earl Nightingale.
You will either step forward into growth, or you will step back into
safety.   —Abraham Maslow

Problems

Every garden presents innumerable fascinating problems.
                                                —Winston Churchill

You must never, even for a second, let yourself think that you can
fail. Thinking is the hardest work there is, which is the probable
reason why so few engage in it.   —Henry Ford

If you have a job without aggravations, you don't have a job.
                                                —Malcolm Forbes

On Lessons

Life is not a continuum of pleasant choices, but of inevitable problems that call for strength, determination, and hard work.

—Indian proverb

Think Walks

Half the interest of a garden is the constant exercise of the imagination.- —Maria Theresa Earle

The moment my legs begin to move, my thoughts begin to flow.

—Henry David Thoreau

All truly great thoughts are conceived by walking. Never trust a thought that didn't come by walking. —Friedrich Nietzsche.

We should take wandering outdoor walks so that the mind might be nourished and refreshed by the open air and deep breathing.

—Seneca

I have walked myself into my best thoughts, and I know of no thought so burdensome that one cannot walk away from it. Thus if one just keeps on walking, everything will be all right.

—Kierkegaard

Prudence

A prudent man doesn't make the goat his gardener.

On Lessons

—Hungarian proverb

Wisely and slow. They stumble that run fast.   —Shakespeare

All enterprises which are entered on with indiscreet zeal may be pursued with great vigour at first, but are sure to collapse in the end.
                                                                —Tacitus

It is better to be careful a hundred times than to be killed once.
                                                                —Unknown

Think like a man of action, act like a man of thought.
                                                                –Henri Bergson.

I think we should follow a simple rule. If we can take the worst, take the risk.   —Dr. Joyce Brothers

Essentialism

If you spread the water across many, many seeds, you don't have as much water for one seed.   —Tyler Perry

Deciding what not to do is as important as deciding what to do.
                                                                —Steve Jobs

The essence of strategy is choosing what not to do.
                                                                —Michael Porter

On Lessons

I suggest that you become obsessed about the things you want. Otherwise, you're going to spend a lifetime being obsessed with making up excuses as to why you didn't get the life you wanted.

—Grant Cardone

The difference between successful people and really successful people is that really successful people say no to almost everything.

—Warren Buffett

Flexible Plans

There are no gardening mistakes, only experiments.

—Janet Kilburn Phillips

All failure is failure to adapt, all success is successful adaptation.

—Max McKeown

Intelligence is the ability to adapt to change.　　—Stephen Hawking

Adapt or perish, now as ever, is nature's inexorable imperative.

—H. G. Wells.

All you need is the plan, the road map, and the courage to press on to your destination.　　—Earl Nightingale

It's never too late, in fiction or in life, to revise.　　— Nancy Thayer

It's always your next move.　　—Napoleon Hill

Learning Curves

Gardening is learning, learning, learning. That's the fun of them. You're always learning. —Helen Mirren

If you are not willing to learn, no one can help you. If you are determined to learn, no one can stop you. —Brian Tracy

To earn more you must learn more. —Robin Sharma

An investment in knowledge always pays the best interest. —Benjamin Franklin

We've actually tracked senior leaders here at Vanguard and asked why some did better in the long run than others. I used to use the word 'complacency' to describe the ones that didn't work out. But the more I reflect on it, the more I realize that's not quite it . . . The people who have continued to be successful here have stayed on a growth trajectory. They just keep surprising you with how much they're growing. —Bill McNabb

In this world, you have to learn how to learn and get in the habit of always wanting to learn. Most people won't put in the time to get a knowledge advantage. —Mark Cuban

Self-Mastery

A man sooner or later discovers that he is the master-gardener of his soul, the director of his life.   —James Allen

Achieve self-mastery over your thoughts, and constantly direct them toward your goals and objectives. Learn to focus your attention on the goals that you want to achieve and on finding ways to achieve those goals.   —Napoleon Hill

Be as you wish to seem.   —Socrates

Hold your goal before you; everything else will take care of itself.
                    —Earl Nightingale

Act, look, feel successful, conduct yourself accordingly, and you will be amazed at the positive results.   —William James

I am, indeed, a king, because I know how to rule myself.
                    —Pietro Aretino

Self-control is the quality that distinguishes the fittest to survive.
                    —George Bernard Shaw

Remarkability

If you've never experienced the joy of accomplishing more than you can imagine, plant a garden.   —Robert Brault

The key to finding your remarkability is to think about what makes you surprising, interesting, or novel. —Mark Schaefer

Be so good they can't ignore you. —Steve Martin

By definition, remarkable things get remarked upon. Remarkable doesn't mean remarkable to you. It means remarkable to me. Am I going to make a remark about it? If not, then you're average.
—Seth Godin

Leverage

To dream a garden and then to plant it is an act of independence and even defiance to the greater world. —Stanley Crawford

No issue can be negotiated unless you first have the clout to compel negotiation. —Saul Alinsky

You never get what you deserve, but only what you have the leverage to negotiate. —Jalen Rose

Sociability

The very best relationship has a gardener and a flower. The gardener nurtures and the flower blooms. —Carole Radziwill

Your career success in the workplace of today, independent of technical expertise, depends on the quality of your people skills.

On Lessons

—Harold M. Messmer Jr.

I think the lie we've told people in the marketplace is that a degree
gets you a job. A degree doesn't get you a job. What gets you a job is
the ability to carry yourself into that room and shake a hand and look
someone in the eye and have people skills. These are the things that
cause people to become successful.   —Dave Ramsey

Social intelligence is the key to career and life success . . . It is
referred to as 'tact,' 'common sense,' and 'street smarts.'
                                        —Ronald E. Riggio, PhD.

Recognition is a short-term need that has to be satisfied on an
ongoing basis—weekly, maybe daily.
                                                —Jim Harter

There are two things people want more than sex and money . . .
recognition and praise.   —Mary Kay Ash

Begin with praise and honest appreciation.   —Dale Carnegie

People will forget what you said and did, but they will never forget
how you made them feel.   —Carl W. Buehner

Sour Adversity

The strongest oak of the forest is not one that is protected from the
storm and hidden from the sun. It's the one that stands in the open
where it is compelled to struggle for its existence against the winds
and rains and the scorching sun.   —Napoleon Hill

On Lessons

Doing what's right's no guarantee against misfortune.

—William McFee

Faced with crisis, the man of character falls back upon himself.

—Charles de Gaulle

In times of adversity and change, we really discover who we are and what we're made of.   —Howard Schultz

Every adversity carries within it the seed of an equal or greater benefit.   —Napoleon Hill

Let me embrace thee, sour adversity, for wise men say it is the wisest course.   —Shakespeare

Acquiescence

If you enjoy the fragrance of a rose, you must accept the thorns which it bears.   —Isaac Hayes

Expecting that life is hard and accepting that ultimately results in it being less painful. We can't necessarily get rid of pain, including the pain of losing a job or having to move, but we can get rid of suffering, and suffering is failing to accept what is.   —Stephen Josephson, PhD.

Suffering is basically the mind's refusal to accept reality as it is.

—Marcus Thomas

On Lessons

Accept—then act. Whatever the present moment contains, accept it as if you had chosen it . . . This will miraculously transform your whole life.   —Eckhart Tolle

Expecting the world to treat you fairly because you are a good person is a little like expecting the bull not to attack you because you're a vegetarian.   —Dennis Wholey

Wisdom . . . is knowing what you have to accept.   —Wallace Stegner

The resistance to the unpleasant situation is the root of suffering.
                                        —Ram Dass

Acceptance of what has happened is the first step to overcoming the consequences of any misfortune.   —William James

Emotional Guidance

Wise is the person whose heart and mind listen to what Nature says. Time will tell, but we often fail to listen.   —Michael p. Garofalo

Feelings are really your GPS system for life. When you're supposed to do something, or not supposed to do something, your emotional guidance system lets you know.   —Oprah Winfrey

A lot of what passes for depression these days is nothing more than a body saying that it needs work.   —Geoffrey Norman

For the past thirty-three years, I have looked in the mirror every morning and asked myself: 'If today were the last day of my life, would I want to do what I'm about to do today?' And whenever the answer has been 'no' for too many days in a row, I know I need to change something.   —Steve Jobs

Whenever you feel stressed, anxious, worried or uneasy about any part of your life, it's nature's way of telling you that something is wrong. It's a message that there's something that you need to address or deal with. There's something that you need to do more or less of. There's something that you need to get into or out of. Very often you'll suffer from what has been called 'divine discontent.' You'll find dread in your days.   —Brian Tracy

Accountability

Life is a garden. You reap what you sow. -   —Paulo Coelho

It is a painful thing to look at your own trouble and know that you yourself, and no one else, has made it.   —Sophocles

Mistakes fail in their mission of helping the person who blames them on the other fellow.   —Henry S. Haskins

The fault, dear Brutus, is not in our stars, but in ourselves.
                                         —Shakespeare

Ninety-nine percent of the failures come from people who have the habit of making excuses.   —George Washington Carver

You always succeed in producing a result.   —Tony Robbins

We are all self-made, but only the successful will admit it.

—Earl Nightingale

Direction

One of the most delightful things about a garden is the anticipation it
provides. —W. E. Johns

The road is always better than the inn. —Cervantes

Know what you want to do, hold the thought firmly, and do everyday
what should be done, and every sunset will see you that much nearer
the goal. —Elbert Hubbard

We must not . . . ignore the small daily differences we can make
which, over time, add up to big differences that we often cannot
foresee. —Marian Wright Edelman

Nobody made a greater mistake than he who did nothing because he
could do only a little. —Edmund Burke

Success is the sum of small efforts, repeated day in and day out.

—Robert Collier

One thing at a time, all things in succession . . . That which grows
slowly endures. —Josiah Gilbert Holland

Happiness is a direction, not a place. —Sydney J. Harris

It is by attempting to reach the top at a single leap that so much misery is produced in the world. —William Cobbett

Plodding wins the race. —Aesop

I find the great thing in this world is not so much where we stand, as in what direction we are moving. —Oliver Wendell Holmes Jr.

Self-Discipline

Every garden is a chore sometimes, but no real garden is nothing but a chore. —Nancy Grasby

The one quality which sets one man apart from another—the key which lifts one to every aspiration while others are caught up in the mire of mediocrity—is not talent, formal education, nor intellectual brightness. It is self-discipline. With self-discipline, all things are possible. Without it, even the simplest goal can seem like the most impossible dream. —Theodore Roosevelt

Success is a comfort awarded only to those willing to do the uncomfortable. Growth requires a constant state of discomfort so get used to it. —Darren Hardy

Resolve to perform what you ought. Perform without fail what you resolve. —Benjamin Franklin

Live like no one else now, so later you can live and give like no one else. —Dave Ramsey

On Lessons

A professional is someone who can do his best work when he doesn't feel like it.　　　　　　　　　　　　　　　—Alistair Cooke

The ability to delay gratification in the short term in order to enjoy greater rewards in the long term is the indispensable prerequisite for success.　　　　　　　　　　　　　　　—Brian Tracy

Small disciplines repeated with consistency every day, lead to great achievements gained slowly over time.　　　　—John C. Maxwell

Your ability to discipline yourself to set clear goals, and then to work toward them every day will do more to guarantee your success than any other single factor.　　　　　　　　　　—Brian Tracy

We must all suffer one of two pains: the pain of discipline or the pain of regret.　　　　　　　　　　　　　　　—Jim Rohn

Impact Statistics

Don't judge each day by the harvest you reap, but by the seeds that you plant.　　　　　　　　　　　　　　　—Anonymous

Nothing is easier than self-deceit.　　　　　—Demosthenes

Follow effective action with quiet reflection. From the quiet reflection will come even more effective action.　　　—Peter Drucker

Asking

Because a garden means constantly making choices, it offers almost limitless possibilities for surprise and satisfaction.　　—Jane Garmey

You get in life what you have the courage to ask for. Ask for what you want! Give other people the opportunity to say 'yes.' Stop saying 'no' for them.　　　　　　　　　　　　　　　　—Oprah Winfrey

Learn to ask for what you want. The worst people can do is not give you what you ask for which is precisely where you were before you asked.　　　　　　　　　　　　　　—Peter McWilliams

Many things are lost for want of asking.　　　—English proverb

If you don't go after what you want, you'll never have it. If you don't ask, the answer is always no. If you don't step forward, you're always in the same place.　　　　　　　　　　　　　—Nora Roberts

Affluence

Watching something grow is good for morale. It helps us believe in life.　　　　　　　　　　　　　　　　—Myron S. Kaufman

Thrift is not an affair of the pocket but an affair of character.
　　　　　　　　　　　　　　　　　　　　—S. W. Straus

Men who make money rarely saunter; men who save money rarely swagger.　　　　　　　　　　　　　—Edward Bulwer-Lytton

A bank is a place that will lend you money if you can prove that you
don't need it   —Bob Hope

"Each day acquire something to fortify you against poverty, against
death.   —Seneca

Try to save something while your salary is small; it's impossible to
save after you begin to earn more.   —Jack Benny

Money is a very excellent servant, but a terrible master.
       —P. T. Barnum

If your outgo exceeds your income, then your upkeep will be your
downfall.   —Bill Earle

Wealth is power. With wealth many things are possible.
       —George S. Clason

Self-Forgiveness

A gardener learns more in the mistakes than in the successes.
      —Barbara Dodge Borland

If your compassion does not include yourself, it is incomplete.
       —Buddha

Forgive yourself for your faults and your mistakes and move on.
       —Les Brown

Forgive yourself for not having the foresight to know what now
seems so obvious in hindsight.   —Judy Belmont

As I walked out the door toward the gate that would lead to my
freedom, I knew if I didn't leave my bitterness and hatred behind, I'd
still be in prison . . . Forgiveness liberates the soul.

—Nelson Mandela

There are many aspects to success. Material wealth is only one
component . . . But success also includes good health, energy and
enthusiasm for life, fulfilling relationships, creative freedom,
emotional and psychological stability, a sense of well-being, and
peace of mind.   —Deepak Chopra

Success Habits

Habits are like a garden full of seeds. Some grow into flowers; others
into weeds.   —Marie Ciota

All bad habits start slowly and gradually, and before you know you
have the habit, the habit has you.   —Zig Ziglar

Motivation is what gets you started. Habit is what keeps you going.

—Jim Rohn

Once you understand that habits can change, you have the freedom
and the responsibility to remake them. Once you understand that

habits can be rebuilt, the power of habit becomes easier to grasp,
and the only option left is to get to work.　　　—Charles Duhigg

Think Wealth

He who hunts for flowers will find flowers; and he who loves weeds
will find weeds.　　　　　　　　　　—Henry Ward Beecher

You must walk to the beat of a different drummer, the same beat
that the wealthy hear. If the beat sounds normal, evacuate the dance
floor immediately! The goal is to not be normal, because normal is
broke.　　　　　　　　　　　　　　—Dave Ramsey

All riches have their origin in Mind.　　　　　Robert Collier

Keep your best wishes close to your heart and watch what happens.
　　　　　　　　　　　　　　　　—Tony DeLiso

A prosperity consciousness attracts money like iron filings to a
magnet.　　　　　　　　　　　　　—Brian Tracy

If you would be wealthy, think of saving as well as getting.
　　　　　　　　　　　　　　　—Benjamin Franklin

The wealthy buy luxuries last, while the poor and middle-class tend
to buy luxuries first.　　　　　　　　—Robert Kiyosaki

Lack of money means discomfort, means squalid worries, means
shortage of tobacco, means ever-present consciousness of failure—
above all, it means loneliness.　　　　　—George Orwell

Like Warren, I had a considerable passion to get rich, not because I wanted Ferraris—I wanted the independence. I desperately wanted it.   — Charlie Munger

Frugality

By sowing frugality we reap liberty, a golden harvest.   —Agesilaus

One cannot both feast and become rich.   —Ashanti proverb

Beware of little expenses; a small leak will sink a great ship.
                                                    —Benjamin Franklin

In the old days, a person who saved money was a miser; nowadays, the same person is a wonder.   —Anonymous

Allocating time and money in the pursuit of looking superior often has a predictable outcome: inferior economic achievement.
                                                    —Thomas J. Stanley

What are three words that profile the affluent? FRUGAL FRUGAL FRUGAL.   — Thomas J. Stanley

Profitability

Wealth, like a tree, grows from a tiny seed.   —George S. Clason

He that will not economize will have to agonize.   —Confucius

Work is a surefire money-making scheme.   —Dave Ramsey

Without labor nothing prospers.   —Sophocles

A television costs you about $40,000 a yea—not to own it, but to watch it. What else could you do with that time?   —Jim Rohn

Get Out of Debt

Interest on debts grows without rain.   —Yiddish proverb

Today, there are three kinds of people: the haves, the have-nots, and the have-not-paid-for-what-they-haves.   —Earl Wilson

Debt is the worst poverty.   —Magnus Gottfried Lichtwer

A man in debt is so far a slave.   —Ralph Waldo Emerson

The greatest enemy of financial well-being is not poverty but debt.   —Kent Nerburn

It is the debtor that is ruined by hard times.   —Rutherford B. Hayes

I owe, I owe, so off to work I go.   —Dave Ramsey

Getting out and staying out of debt is key. Debt is the biggest barrier, a parasite to wealth.   —Ann Wilson

Save Urgently

It is only the farmer who faithfully plants seed in the spring who reaps a harvest in the autumn. —B. C. Forbes

Save money and money will save you. —Jamaican proverb

If you wish to get rich, save what you get. A fool can earn money; but it takes a wise man to save and dispose of it to his own advantage.
—Brigham Young

If you cannot save money, the seeds of greatness are not in you.
—Clement Stone

Keep Score

If we are unhappy with the harvest we're reaping, we should sow different seed. —Phil Pringle

What gets measured gets done. —Tom Peters

What gets measured gets managed. —Peter Drucker

What gets measured gets improved. —Robin Sharma

Make it a policy to know your net worth to the penny. Focus on all four of your net worth factors: increasing your income, increasing your savings, increasing your investment returns, and decreasing your cost of living by simplifying your lifestyle —T. Harv Eker

If investing is entertaining, if you're having fun, you're probably not making any money. Good investing is boring.   –George Soros

Investing should be more like watching paint dry or watching grass grow. If you want excitement, take $800 and go to Las Vegas.
                                                    —Paul Samuelson

Minimize Risk

Agriculture will always have changes, always have a set of risks.
                                                    —Wright Morton

Smart people do dumb things. People are trying to be smart—all I am trying to do is not to be an idiot, but it's harder than most people think.   —Charlie Munger

Rule No. 1: Never lose money. Rule No. 2:Never forget Rule No. 1.
                                                    —Warren Buffett

I hate to be the bearer of bad news but great investing is boring. I mean like really boring.   —David Rae

Do not take yearly results too seriously. Instead, focus on four-or five-year averages.   —Benjamin Graham

Most investors, both institutional and individual, will find that the best way to own common stocks is through an index fund that charges minimal fees.   —Warren Buffett

Multiply It

A grain of corn placed in fertile soil shoots up a green stalk, blossoms and produces an ear of corn containing hundreds of grains, each capable of doing what the one grain did. —R. H. Jarrett

The big money is not in the buying and selling. But in the waiting. Most people are too fretful, they worry too much. Success means being very patient, but aggressive when it's time.

—Charlie Munger

Passive Income

Better to die fighting for freedom than be a prisoner all the days of your life. —Bob Marley

What is freedom? Freedom is the right to choose: the right to create for oneself the alternatives of choice. —Archibald MacLeish

You become financially free when your passive income exceeds your expenses. —T. Harv Eker

If you don't find a way to make money while you sleep, you will work until you die. —Warren Buffett

Residual income is passive income that comes in every month whether you show up or not. It's when you no longer get paid on your personal efforts alone . . . It's one of the keys to financial freedom." —Steve Fisher

To obtain financial freedom, one must be either a business owner, an investor, or both, generating passive income, particularly on a monthly basis.   —Robert Kiyosaki

PART V: ON HAPPINESS

Money and Happiness

Money isn't everything...but it ranks right up there with oxygen.
—Rita Davenport

Money is a headache, and money is the cure.   —Terri Guillemets

Money can't buy happiness, but neither can poverty.   —Leo Rosten

I know money isn't everything. but it certainly is something.
—Thisuri Wanniarachchi

When I was young, I thought that money was the most important thing in life; now that I am old I know that it is.   –Oscar Wilde

It's pretty hard to tell what does bring happiness; poverty and wealth have both failed.   –Kin Hubbard

Having money is a way of being free of money.   –Albert Camus

Lack of money is the root of all evil.   —George Bernard Shaw

Money isn't everything. It's just most everything.   —Nica Clark

Without prosperity the fullness of human happiness is not possible.
—Sunday Adelaja

Money is better than poverty, if only for financial reasons
—Woody Allen

Money can't buy happiness, but it can buy you the kind of misery you
prefer.   —Spike Milligan

Whoever said money can't buy happiness simply didn't know where
to go shopping.   —Bo Derek

Money won't make you happy . . . But everybody wants to find out
for them-selves   Zig Ziglar

Money isn't the most important thing in life, but it's reasonably close
to oxygen on the gotta have it scale.   –Zig Ziglar

It's just as easy to be happy with a lot of money as with a little.
                                                           —Marvin Traub

Poverty is like punishment for a crime you didn't commit.
                                                           —Eli Khamarov

Money isn't everything – but it's a long way ahead of what comes
next.   –Edmund Stockdale

There are only 2 paths to happiness in life. Utter Stupidity or
Exceptional Wealth.   —Ziad K. Abdelnour

Annual income twenty pounds, annual expenditure nineteen six,
result happiness. Annual income twenty pounds, annual expenditure
twenty pound ought and six, result misery.   —Charles Dickens

The way taxes are, you might as well marry for love.
                                                           —Joe E. Lewis

ON HAPPINESS

It pays to get rich.   Ashleigh Brilliant

It is true that money cannot buy happiness, but it does make it
possible for you to enjoy the best that the world has to offer.
                                        —George S. Clason

I guess money can't buy happiness if you shop in the wrong places.
                                        —Nora Roberts

When a fellow says it ain't the money but the principle of the thing,
it's the money.   –Artemus Ward

Happiness is not bought by money, but it can buy circumstances and
conditions that improve the chances of a worldly kind of happiness.
                                        —Steve Scott

Money, if it doesn't bring you happiness, will at least help you be
miserable in comfort.   —Helen Gurley

Money doesn't make you happy. I now have $50 mil-lion but I was
just as happy when I had only $48 million.
                                        —Arnold Schwarzenegger

I wish I were either rich enough or poor enough to do a lot of things
that are impossible in my present comfortable circumstances.
                                        —Don Hebold

Car sickness is the feeling you get when the monthly car payment is
due.   —Unknown

ON HAPPINESS

Money can't buy happiness, but it can buy a huge yacht that sails
right next to it.   –David Lee Roth

Money is like a sixth sense—and you can't make use of the other five
without it.   —William Somerset Maugham

Money is the currency of life because it is the external measurement
system that all of us have as to how we judge where we are in our
own lives.   Suze Orman

Although wealth may not bring happiness, the immediate prospect of
it provides a wonderfully close imitation.   —Patrick O'Brian

There is no such thing as being too independent.   –Victoria Billings

Another advantage of being rich is that all your faults are called
eccentricities.   —Anonymous

Women prefer men who have something tender about them—
especially the legal kind.   —Kay Ingram

Prosperity gathers smiles, while adversity scatters them.
                                        —William Scott Downey

In my day, we didn't have self-esteem, we had self-respect, and no
more of it than we had earned.   –Jane Haddam

How little a thing can make us happy when we feel that we have
earned it.   Mark Twain

ON HAPPINESS

I am having an out of money experience.   —Unknown

You can never have too much money.   –Jess C. Scott

There are two primary choices in life; to accept conditions as they exist or accept responsibility for changing them.
                                                          —Denis Waitley

Happiness comes only when we push our brains and hearts to the farthest reaches of which we are capable.   —Leo C. Rosten

It is not the settled life that we should pursue but the satisfying and useful life.   –the wealthy gardener

Contentment is not happiness. An oyster may be contented. Happiness is com-pounded of richer elements.   –Christian Bovee

If you deliberately plan on being less than you can capable of being, then I warn you that you will be unhappy for the rest of your life.
                                                          —Abraham Maslow

I am sure in my own mind that the one business of life is to succeed, that God did not give us these magnificent brains, these miraculous personalities, and these wonderful physical qualities and then expect us to waste our lives in failure.   –Sterling W. Sill

I want to get even. I want to get even more money.   –Jarod Kintz

The only liberty an inferior man really cherishes is the liberty to quit work, stretch out in the sun, and scratch himself.   –H.L. Mencken

Money and Peace of Mind

Having money is a way of being free of money .   —Albert Camus

Wealth does not necessarily mean having millions and millions of pesos. Being wealthy simply means having the financial resources to support your chosen life-style. Wealth is nothing more than having money to fund your particular needs at any given time.

—Francisco Colayco

Although money alone won't make us happy, the lack of money surely will make us miserable.

—Suze Orman

You must gain control over your money or the lack of it will forever control you.   —Dave Ramsey

Money does not make you happy but it quiets the nerves.

—Sean O'Casey

Money is the sixth sense that makes it possible to enjoy the other five.   —Richard Ney

Money's only important when you don't have any.   –Sting

Money is human happiness in the abstract.

—Arthur Schopenhauer

A hundred load of worry will not pay an ounce of debt.

—George Herbert

Self-reliance is the only road to true freedom and being one's own person is its ultimate reward.   Patricia Sampson

Worry bankrupts the spirit.   —Terri Guillemets

It's easier to feel a little more spiritual with a couple of bucks in your pocket.   –Craig Ferguson

Money can't buy happiness, but it certainly is a stress reliever.
                    —Besa Kosova

It is not work that kills men; it is worry. Work is healthy; you can hardly put more up-on a man than he can bear.
                    —Henry Ward Beecher

Poverty is a great enemy to human happiness; it certainly destroys liberty, and it makes some virtues impracticable, and others extremely difficult.   —Samuel Johnson

Peace of mind is attained not by ignoring problems, but by solving them.   –Raymond Hull

No, my son, do not aspire for wealth and labor not only to be rich. Strive instead for happiness, to be loved and to love, and most important to acquire peace of mind and serenity.   —Og Mandino

Owning a home is a keystone of wealth, both financial affluence and emotional security.   —Suze Orman

Success is peace of mind which is a direct result of self-satisfaction in knowing you did your best to become the best you are capable of becoming.　　　　　　　　　　　　　　　—John Wooden

Financial peace isn't the acquisition of stuff. It's learning to live on less than you make, so you can give money back and have money to invest. You can't win until you do this.　　　　　—Dave Ramsey

As a cure for worrying, work is better than whiskey.
—Thomas A. Edison

If you're doing your best, you won't have any time to worry about failure.　　　　　　　　　　　　　　—H. Jackson Brown, Jr.

That man is blest who does his best and leaves the rest; do not worry.　　　　　　　　　　　　　　　　—Charles Deems

Money and Service

In about the same degree as you are helpful, you will be happy.
　　　　　　　　　　　　　　　　　　　—Karl Reiland

The human contribution is the essential ingredient.
　　　　　　　　　　　　　　　　—Ethel Percy Andrus

Show me a person whose chief aim is happiness, and I'll show you an unhappy person getting nothing done.　　—the Wealthy Gardener

In idleness there is a perpetual despair.　　　—Thomas Carlyle

ON HAPPINESS

A useless life is an early death.   —Goethe

The way to be nothing is to do nothing.   —Nathaniel Howe

The only way to enjoy any-thing in this life is to earn it first.
                                                        —Ginger Rogers

Whoever renders service to many puts himself in line for greatness—
great wealth, great return, great satisfaction, great reputation, and
great joy.   —Jim Rohn

Labor, if it were not necessary for existence, would be indispensable
for the happiness of man.   —Samuel Johnson

Business is the art of extracting money from another man's pocket
without resorting to violence.   –Max Amsterdam

We will receive not what we idly wish for but what we justly earn.
Our rewards will always be in exact proportion to our service.
                                                    —Earl Nightingale

Service to others is the rent you pay for your room here on earth.
                                                    —Mohammed Ali

Continuity of purpose is one of the most essential ingredients of
happiness in the long run, and for most men this comes chiefly
through their work.   —Bertrand Russell

Wherever a man turns he can find someone who needs him.
                                                    —Albert Schweitzer

The quality of your work, in the long run, is the deciding factor on how much your services are valued by the world.

—Orison Swett Marden

That is no higher religion than human service. To work for the common good is the greatest creed.　　　　—Woodrow Wilson

The purpose of human life is to serve, and to show compassion and the will to help others.　　　　—Albert Schweitzer

Find a need and fill it.　　　　—Ruth Stafford Peale

The few who do are the envy of the many who only watch.

—Jim Rohn

Deliver more than you are getting paid to do. The victory of success will be half won when you learn the secret of putting out more than is expected in all that you do.　　　　—Og Mandino

The success combination in business is: Do what you do better... and: Do more of what you do.　　　　—David J. Schwartz

My experience indicates that most people who've accumulated a great deal of wealth haven't had that as their goal at all. Wealth is only a by-product, not the original motivation.　　　—Michael Milken

When I got my life on purpose and focused on giving of myself and everything that arrived into my life, then I was prosperous.

—Wayne Dyer

ON HAPPINESS

A business is simply an idea to make other people's lives better.

—Richard Branson

The only way to excellence is to consistently improve yourself every single day.

—Thomas J. Vilord

Everyone should find his or her particular niche in the world's work, where both material prosperity and happiness in abundance may be found.

–Napoleon Hill

When we pursue the aim of accumulation, our service to others must involve two questions: (1) how can I help? and (2) what's in it for me? When we figure out the proper balance between the two, we find a way that leads to financial power.

—the wealthy gardener

Just make up your mind at the very outset that your work is going to stand for quality... that you are going to stamp a superior quality upon everything that goes out of your hands, that what-ever you do shall bear the hallmark of excellence.

–Orison Swett Marden

Never complain about your troubles; they are responsible for more than half your income.

—Robert Updegraff

Quality is never an accident; it is always the result of high intention, sincere effort, intelligent direction, and skillful execution; it represents the wise choice of many alternatives.

—William A Foster

There's no traffic jam on the extra mile.

—Unknown

If at first you don't succeed, you're running about average.

—M.H. Alderson

It's not the employer who pays the wages. Employers only handle the money. It's the customer who pays the wages.　　　—Henry Ford

There is only one boss. The customer. And he can fire everybody in the company from the chairman on down, simply by spending his money somewhere else.　　　—Sam Walton

The entire population, with one trifling exception, is composed of others.　　　–John Andrew Holmes

If you focus on success, you'll have stress. But if you pursue excellence, success will be guaranteed.　　　—Deepak Chopra

The heart that gives, gathers.　　　—Marianne Moor

Step by step, little by little, bit by bit–that is the way to wealth.
—Charles Buxton

People who have accomplished work worthwhile have had a very high sense of the way to do things. They have not been content with mediocrity. They have not confined themselves to the beaten tracks; they have never been satisfied to do things just as others so them, but always a little better. They always pushed things that came to their hands a little higher up, this little farther on, that counts in the quality of life's work. It is constant effort to be first-class in everything one at-tempts that conquers the heights of excellence.
　　　—Orison Swett Marden

Abundance is the quality of life you live and quality of life you give to others.　　　J.K. Rowling

It's easy to make a buck. It's a lot tougher to make a difference.

—Tom Brokaw

I'm a millionaire, I'm a multi-millionaire. I'm filthy rich. You know why I'm a multi-millionaire? Cause multi-millions like what I do.

—Michael Moore

More Resources

Quotes in this book are from
*The Wealthy Gardener: Lessons on Prosperity
between Father and Son.*

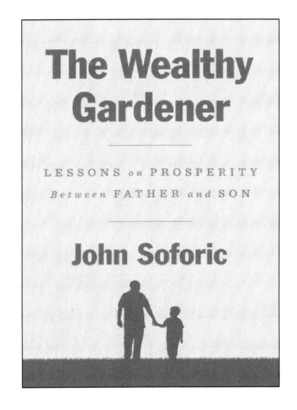

The sequel to The Wealthy Gardener, the apprentice becomes the master. Jimmy teaches the troubled teens a system of 12 essential rules so they can succeed financially and be free in five years.

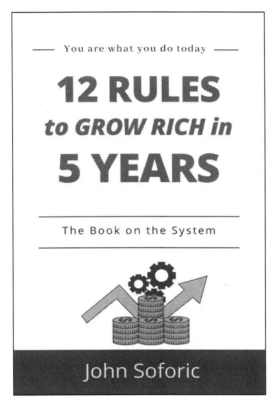

Available on Amazon

The Wealthy BookHeads

wealthybookheads.com

The website is under development, and will be a learning resource with videos, book reviews, author interviews, and a weekly podcast.

WealthyBookHeads.com

About John Soforic

I wrote *The Wealthy Gardener* for my son in college. I wanted to distill my own lessons about wealth after I gained financial freedom. I never imagined the book would sell 100,000 copies, be translated into 10 foreign languages, hit the top 50 worldwide on audible, and be purchased by a New York publisher. If you want to keep in touch, check out wealthybookheads.com. I hope to shine a light on the best books and authors that I think are worth your attention.

Made in the USA
Columbia, SC
10 February 2025